AF804026

Parallel Processing with Communicating Process Architecture

Parallel Processing
with Communicating Process Architecture

Ian East
University of Buckingham

UCL
PRESS

© Ian East 1995

This book is copyright under the Berne Convention.
No reproduction without permission.
All rights reserved.

First published in 1995 by UCL Press

UCL Press Limited
University College London
Gower Street
London WC1E 6BT

The name of University College London (UCL) is a registered trade mark used by UCL Press with the consent of the owner.

British Library Cataloguing-in-Publication Data
A CIP catalogue record for this book is available from the British Library.

ISBN: 1-85728-239-6 PB

This book has been typeset, proofed, and passed for press by the author.

Typeset in Palatino and Gill Sans.
Printed and bound by
Page Bros (Norwich) Ltd, England.

Ideas are born of love, not of labour.

Table of Contents

Preface

Why is parallel processing so widely regarded as a difficult subject, to be addressed only at an advanced phase in a computing curriculum? The explanation for this perceived difficulty seems to arise not from any inherent complexity, but simply from the history of the development of processors and their programming. The enormous momentum that results from commercial exploitation of existing systems and methods perpetuates the myth. Had history been different, it might well be the other way around. Systems constrained to run *without* concurrency might instead be perceived to be difficult to design and as unnatural as they indeed are.

It should be remembered that artificial devices for processing information have been around for hundreds, perhaps thousands, of years. Only a new implementation technology has permitted rapid exploration of how information may be processed by machine. Over the 50 years in which people have been building electronic information processors, progress has been so persistent that we have all come to expect it to continue indefinitely. But it did not take long before the limit to the speed with which each datum could be processed became decided by the *implementation* technology alone. Apart from improving that technology, the only way to progress was to process data in parallel. However, the introduction of parallelism went unnoticed by programmers because programming itself went unchanged. Processor architects took responsibility for implementing parallelism. They did so in just the same way that an assembly line improves production in a factory. The translation of program instructions is now performed using a *pipeline* of subordinate processors.

Two problems exist with this approach. First, only a modest proportion of the parallelism possible in a given process may be extracted from a purely serial program. Secondly, there is a strict limit to the parallelism achievable, equal to the length of the pipeline. In short, it will only get you so far.

Two options exist for programming a network of parallel processors. Either parallelism is rendered *explicit* or it must be *implicit*. If explicit then distinct sub-programs describe the behaviour of each processor. If implicit then translation must expose the parallelism to the machine. I draw no conclusion about which is better, though any decision must pay respect to the application concerned. On the other hand, understanding may only be acquired while remaining close to the machine being programmed. After all, even if parallelism is to be implicit, *someone* has to design and compose the compiler. That is why this book is about (explicit) parallel programming.

Parallel programming requires a parallel programming language. I make no apology for the choice of occam™ for the purposes of illustration. It offers synchronous communication as a primitive of the procedure metaphor and fulfils the requirements of security and readability which befit a modern programming language. However, this book is not dependent upon occam. It should not be difficult for anyone to translate the code fragments that appear into any appropriate language they choose. occam is far from cryptic. Very few other languages could approach its clarity, simplicity, and elegance.

For a complete description of occam I refer the reader to the reference manual (Inmos 1992). I also very highly recommend an article by Professor Peter Welch (University of Kent) regarding the advantages it offers (Welch 1992). Various compilers are available. Inmos (a member of the SGS Thomson Microelectronics Group) sell a series of toolsets for their transputer products. Perhaps the most versatile tool available is the Southampton Portable occam Compiler (SPOC), which translates occam into C and is available, free of charge, by anonymous FTP from the British Higher Education National Software Archive (HENSA) (`unix.hensa.ac.uk`, `/parallel/occam/compilers/spoc`). The beauty of SPOC is that it removes the need for a compiler dedicated to a particular chosen architecture. Few processors lack a C compiler nowadays.

Underlying the approach taken throughout this book is the theory of Communicating Sequential Processes (CSP) of Professor C. A. R. Hoare FRS of Oxford University (Hoare 1985). CSP departs from the conventional "data-centred" model of computation and focuses instead upon *events*. It has led to the development of a parallel programming methodology which has matured over the last few years and become known as Communicating Process Architecture. Along with a sound underpinning theory (CSP), an expressive modern parallel programming language (occam), and a target processor designed for the role (SGS Thomson Transputer), CPA offers a consistent framework in which to achieve real

---

™ occam is a registered trade mark of Inmos, a member of SGS Thomson Microelectronics Group.

capability in parallel processing without the confusion which may easily result from consideration of the full range of paradigms which exist. My aim is depth rather than breadth. I feel that should someone master this methodology then they will be capable of at least asking the right questions of any other with which they come into contact.

I have already been criticized for not introducing CSP early on and for not presenting many more ideas using its vocabulary. I do not think this is appropriate. In my experience it takes time before students are happy to switch between CSP and `occam` (or any other programming language). Ideas should be first presented in the simplest, and most practical, terms possible. Most people are better at generalization than specialization, which is why illustration is so important, and why powerful theory presented too early can obscure rather than reveal.

In the final chapter, about deadlock avoidance, there was no choice. The need to be absolutely precise, and to be able to offer progressive refinement from design towards implementation, prompted the use of CSP. Much of this material is new and springs from an active research interest, although the use of CSP as a design tool is well established. A bibliography is given which should satisfy the more curious.

I make no apology for brevity. It was never my aim to produce a book rich in case histories to illustrate the principles it documents. As a student myself, I found great value in *concise* volumes that cut to the quick. As an aid in this regard, key ideas are highlighted throughout the book by means of an arrow symbol ("➤"). In any case, it is not really possible to illustrate the principles properly until *all* of them have been addressed. Proper illustration of application does not offer the pretence that one need only be concerned with one issue at a time. Ideally, I would recommend practical work to follow a course of lectures based upon this book. To attempt to design scalable software, free of deadlock, and then implement and configure it to run on real hardware would prove immensely valuable. Alternatively, one might consider the rather cheaper possibility of seminars analyzing the operation and attributes of some existing software, or perhaps human, systems.

Overall, this book should be accessible to anyone who has such knowledge of structured programming and discrete mathematics as would normally be taught in the first year of a computer science curriculum. I sincerely hope that the book finds a broad audience and proves helpful to people who either simply desire the performance benefits offered by parallel processing or seek liberation from a purely serial programming domain.

It is time that parallel programming became more mainstream. I look forward to the day when computer science students are no longer taught the lie that everything is serial. It is not. The world is parallel.

Acknowledgements

I am indebted to those people who organized, and contributed to, the Technical Meetings of the World occam and Transputer Users Group (WoTUG), which now has branches in many countries. As a result of these meetings a great deal of "know-how" has evolved which now forms a very significant capability in parallel processing. These are now the only technical meetings that I know of which retain informality, a sincerely friendly atmosphere, and where people still seem to seek co-operation rather than the unconstructive excess of competition which destroys the joy in technology and threatens progress itself. I always leave feeling that I have learned something.

I wish to thank two people in particular. First, Jeremy Martin (University of Buckingham) who helped a great deal with Chapter 6, including the contribution of original ideas on its subject. Secondly, Professor Peter Welch (University of Kent) who is responsible for many of the ideas related throughout the book. His energy and vitality has invigorated the field for many a year. Without his effort and creativity this book would not have been possible.

I offer my warmest gratitude to the following folk who have spent their precious time reading the manuscript and offering helpful advice and criticism: Professor Peter Welch (University of Kent), Roger Peel (University of Surrey), Peter Strain-Clark (Open University), Andy Forrest (Imperial College), Professor Chris Adams (University of Buckingham), Sabah Jassim (University of Buckingham), and Jeremy Martin (University of Buckingham).

They share the credit but none of the blame.

Bibliography

Hoare, C. A. R. 1985. *Communicating sequential processes*. Englewood Cliffs, New Jersey: Prentice Hall.

Inmos Ltd 1992. *The* occam 2 *reference manual*. Englewood Cliffs, New Jersey: Prentice Hall.

Welch, P. H. 1992. The role and future of occam. In *Transputer applications: progress and prospects*, proceedings of the Transputer Initiative Symposium, M. Jane, R. Fawcett, T. Mawby (eds), 152–169. Amsterdam: IOS Press.

Chapter 1

The Parallel Nature of Systems

1.1 Co-operation

1.1.1 Introduction

People have been thinking about parallel computing for just a few decades. They have been thinking about parallel systems for several thousand years. Even before agriculture, humans were organizing themselves for purposes such as hunting and, of course, violence[1].

It thus seems sensible to consider parallel organization in human systems before considering how a parallel computer system might be organized. The systems referred to are the construction site, the production line, and the supermarket. It should not be surprising that two of these were born in this century since the last few generations have witnessed by far the greatest advances in human organization in history. Our lives are more complicated, more demanding, and more rewarding (arguably) than those of any of our ancestors. All thanks to the application of new technologies, though it would be a big mistake to believe that every new technology is applied, or applied sensibly, as soon as it is invented.

The root of all successful human organization is *co-operation* (not competition, as some would have us believe). In nineteenth- and twentieth-century Britain, social co-operation has been responsible for the introduction of sanitation, potable water distribution, policing, public transport, and communication services. Much further back in history, the village evolved as a means of co-operative food production and defence. It is co-operation that makes civilization possible. Co-operation is made possible by communication and is the principal survival advantage in the evolution of language[2]. Most of the co-operating that we do every day we do subconsciously and without thinking. We are doing it when we queue for something in the supermarket and when we are at work.

The worker analogue for a processor, that of a task for a process, and that of the exchange of messages for process interaction, will prove most valuable later on when we begin addressing parallel software. But for now we shall concern ourselves exclusively with *human* organization in a search for useful ideas. The reader is invited to pause and reflect on systems in his or her own experience and to pose questions. For example, how much management was there and how effective was it?

1.1.2 Fox's Wall

Professor Geoffrey Fox was the first to refer to the simple example of the construction of a wall by a number of workers as a problem in parallel organization. It provides an illustration of all the fundamental methods of breaking a task down into smaller tasks, i.e. of problem *decomposition.*

Figure 1.1 depicts a wall where each brick represents an element of the *domain,* i.e. an indivisible component of the information to be processed.

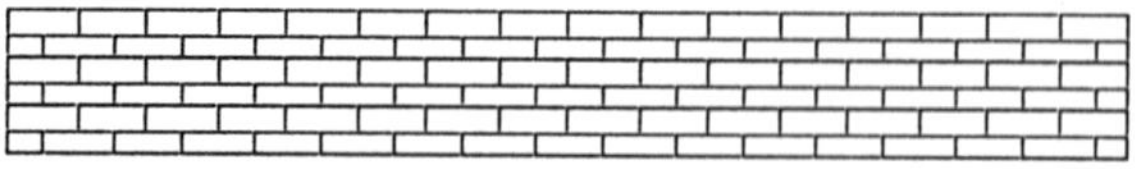

Figure 1.1 Fox's Wall.

The problem is how to get the task done in the shortest possible time with a given number of workers. How do we break down the task? Can we do so in such a way that the workers can just get on with it, without further supervision? Can we do so in such a way that all workers are equally busy? Can we maintain efficiency as either the problem *domain* (the wall) or the workforce grows?

1.1.3 Function decomposition

The first way in which we might try to break down the task is so that each worker performs a distinct function. In the construction of a wall, if we neglect the supply of materials, there are only two functions, that of laying mortar and that of laying bricks. If we now account for material supply then we may add two more functions, that of mixing mortar and that of bringing bricks (assuming an accessible central supply).

Here we meet the two principal disadvantages of function decomposition. First, it is quite likely that there will be fewer tasks than workers. To look at it another way, as many workers as tasks will be required, no fewer and no more. Secondly, some tasks are easier than others. Some workers will be idle some of the time. The system cannot be easily *load-balanced.*

Unfortunately, there are also other objections to function decomposition. We have already stated that if the workforce grows, efficiency will quickly fall as we have no means for the *utilization* of extra workers. This becomes a serious difficulty should the domain grow. Function decomposition fails to offer *scalability* of performance with size of either domain or workforce.

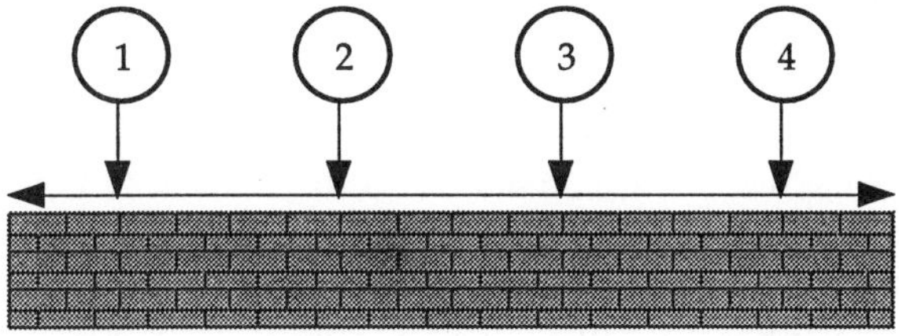

Figure 1.2 Function decomposition of Fox's Wall.

Each worker must have access to the entire domain (each and every brick position). Co-operation must be effected for the laying of each and every brick, as the shading in Figure 1.2 is intended to indicate. One can imagine just how infuriating that would be to the individuals concerned. It is also inefficient.

Function decomposition is often called "demarcation" and results in the requirement of specialized workers who each require individual training, both in how to perform their function and in how to communicate with other workers who will form their environment. This usually results in increased employment and training costs and poor *redundancy*. The failure of just one worker to turn up for work could cause catastrophe. In some systems, such as the emergency services, there has to be redundancy. Such systems still have to operate effectively even when staff are sick.

One might hope for some redeeming feature of function decomposition. This author knows of only one. In systems which can tolerate all the above disadvantages it is possible to exploit the fact that specialized workers may be specially trained to perform their function. Such optimization may be observed on any construction site, although improved tools have now reduced the level of skill which is economically worthwhile.

It should also be added that allocation of tasks to workers may be done just once and without further interference. This is called *static allocation* because it does not change while the job is being done.

1.1.4 Domain decomposition

Perhaps the more obvious, and arguably more simple, approach is to divide the domain by the number of workers available. The scale of the domain allocated per worker is called the *grain size* or *granularity*. This approach does not share the disadvantages of function decomposition.

We are now free to exploit as many workers as we can muster and will maintain the best possible efficiency should the required wall (domain) grow in size. Domain decomposition thus offers scalability. Each worker may easily be given an equal amount of work to do and hence have no excuse for idleness. It is even possible to control the task allocation in such a way as to compensate for performance variation across the workforce and thus get the best out of everyone. Load balancing is therefore straightforward.

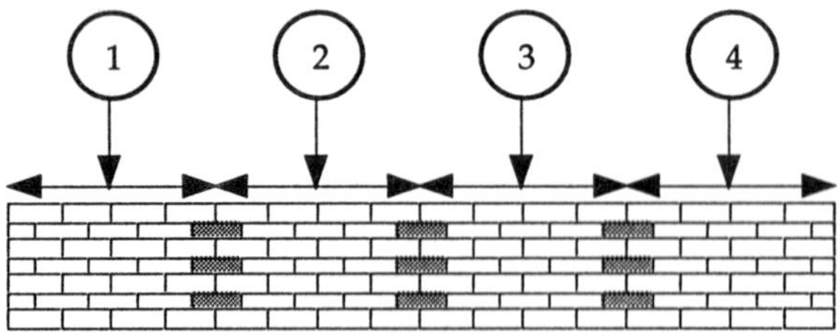

Figure 1.3 Domain decomposition of Fox's Wall.

Workers no longer require access to the entire domain with a consequent gain in efficiency. Co-operation is only required for the laying of the *overlap* between workers (shaded in Fig. 1.3).

Specialization is not required. *Generalized* workers may be employed, which means fewer problems when any are sick. (Nor need the employer be held to ransom by any worker with skills which are hard to come by.) They may all receive the same training which may thus receive more care to perfect. Training materials may be *replicated* to save cost.

Just as function decomposition has a saving grace, so domain decomposition has its limitations. Domain decomposition requires *regularity* in the structure of the domain, *uniformity* of the work requirement, and uniformity of the working capability of the workforce. Too much irregularity, or non-uniformity, and it simply becomes too difficult to decompose the job in such a way as to preserve efficiency.

Given reasonable regularity and uniformity domain decomposition allows static allocation of tasks to workers. However, if these conditions fail, and no efficient function decomposition may be found, then one should turn to *farming*.

1.1.5 Farming

Both domain and function decomposition may lead naturally to algorithms which are purely co-operative *with no management overhead.* Tasks are assigned by static allocation. The term "farming" refers to the repeated farming out of tasks to workers. Initially, each worker is given a task to perform by the farmer. When workers complete tasks they immediately inform the farmer who assigns them new ones. In other words we have *dynamic allocation* of tasks to workers.

Dynamic allocation is required whenever any of the following applies.

- Domain structure is irregular and does not match workforce structure.
- Work required is distributed non-uniformly across domain.
- Work capability is distributed non-uniformly across workforce.
- No distribution of skills exists to match an efficient decomposition of function with static allocation.

A workforce is required for farming, but one with a diversity of skills. For example, for it to work effectively on a construction site one requires workers who are as capable of mixing mortar as they are laying bricks (or fitting door frames, etc.). This makes a suitable workforce more costly than with simple (unmanaged) domain decomposition.

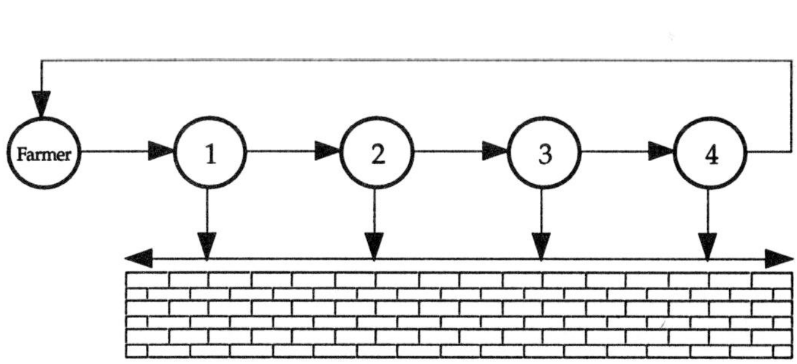

Figure 1.4 Farming with Fox's Wall.

Farming has a recursive definition. The reader should imagine a farm of farms, where farmers are formed effectively into a management hierarchy.

The disadvantage of farming is the management overhead. First, workers are now dedicated to performing functions which are non-productive. Secondly, there must now be extra communication not inherent in the problem, which exists solely to support dynamic allocation of tasks. Worst of all, as the workforce grows there is an increasing communication *bottleneck* at the farmer. The only way to alleviate this is to apply recursion at the cost of having more workers acting as (non-productive) farmers.

A little consideration of the operation of any construction site will make it quickly clear that a task of any complexity is likely to call for a mixture of function *and* domain decomposition. One example is the need to have dedicated workers mixing mortar and fetching bricks, even while a number of identically skilled workers (bricklayers) construct the wall itself by domain decomposition. The example may be extended to encompass the construction of an entire (say) sports complex or office block. Such a mixed decomposition will rarely load balance with static allocation of tasks. Farming will usually then be required.

1.2 Communication

1.2.1 Synchronization

Let us return to the instances of co-operation mentioned earlier with reference to the construction of a wall. When considering function decomposition it was pointed out that co-operation would be required over the laying of each and every brick. One of the advantages of domain decomposition is that it reduces the requirement to one of co-operation only over the laying of bricks in the overlap of sub-domains.

What exactly do workers need to do to effect co-operation? The situation is in fact the same as that encountered when two pedestrians simultaneously wish to pass through a doorway, or when two drivers simultaneously wish to cross a road junction. A *protocol* is required. Two possibilities exist which are applicable to both of these examples. First, there is the competitive "get out of my way, I'm coming through" rule (which seems now to be universal in urban culture). Secondly, there is the co-operative, and hence more successful, "after you" rule.

Both parties have an action they must perform which depends upon that of their neighbour. The actions must be *interleaved* which implies that their *synchronization* must be achieved. Here we meet something fundamental. Co-operation requires communication. Communication requires a protocol.

➤ A protocol is an agreed set of rules for communication.

At very least, a *signal* must be sent. If the "after you" protocol is to be used to govern the access to the shared doorway then all that is required is one party to send a recognizable signal to the other and the problem is solved. Both parties need only agree on the protocol in advance. As children, we learn many such protocols as part of our culture.

Returning to wall construction, it should now be clear how to deal with the overlap (shared domain). A protocol is required. One may easily be designed so that only a signal need be communicated. In reality, human vision will form the *channel* of communication. To make the problem more instructive, the workers will be considered to be blind-folded.

A convenient protocol is to require that each worker send a signal after laying a brick on the sub-domain edge *unless* one is received from the neighbour on that edge. A worker who receives a signal has the duty to lay the next overlapping brick on the corresponding edge. Note that this requires the ability of the worker to distinguish between signals from different neighbours. (A worker with only one effective ear will have a problem!) The reader may wish to experiment with this protocol, perhaps with a friend and a paper and pencil wall.

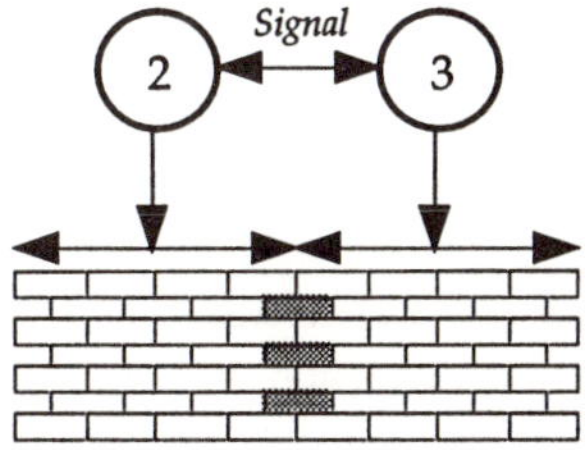

Figure 1.5 Synchronization between workers on horizontally neighbouring sub-domains.

A signal may be considered to be a *message* with no content. Many such signals may be heard on a construction site (not all of which are printable). A typical example might be the shout of "Whoa!" to halt the movement of a length of pipe into position. Again, many such methods are learned by us as children helping our parents maintain the house and car. As part of our cultural tradition, they are widely applicable and thus have considerable economic value.

At a stroke, the need for special co-operation over the laying of particular bricks has been eliminated. A small amount of co-operation is required over the laying of each and every brick. Such an arrangement is known as *lockstep* synchronization because all workers are locked into step, like a military march. There is no longer any need for *shared access* to any part of the domain.

An alternative to the horizontal domain decomposition, shown in Figure 1.5, is vertical domain decomposition. At its simplest, each worker is allocated a single row of brick positions. A little thought will conform that this results in a *pipeline* (as used in a production line). Each worker must iteratively lay a brick and then signal the fellow worker who "owns" the next layer up (Fig. 1.6).

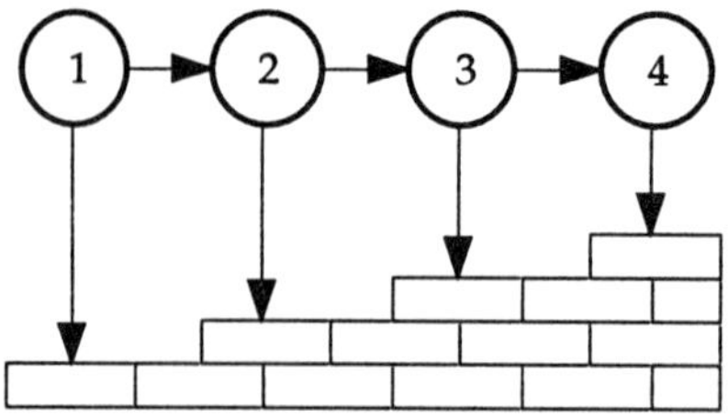

Figure 1.6 Vertical domain decomposition of Fox's Wall (pipeline).

There is a delay before all workers are being utilized which is characteristic of all production lines (pipelines). It is called the *latency* and is a function of the length of the pipeline.

➤ Latency will not diminish efficiency provided that the domain is long with respect to the pipeline.

This can be demonstrated for wall construction. The efficiency for constructing a wall by vertical domain decomposition may be shown to vary with the wall length x and the number of workers n as follows. (It is assumed that there is one worker available for each layer of bricks. The derivation is left as a valuable exercise for the reader.)

$$E = \frac{1}{1 + \frac{3n}{2x}}$$

The two extremes are of interest, that of a very short wall, such that each worker has few bricks to lay, and that of a very long wall, such that each worker has many bricks to lay. The effect of pipeline latency becomes clear.

$$E \propto \frac{x}{n} \qquad (n >> x)$$

$$E \approx 1 \qquad (x >> n)$$

It is clear then that a pipeline is very efficient, and is *scalable*, where the domain extends significantly beyond its length, but is very inefficient when the reverse is true. Thus, the extent of the domain will define the limits to scalability. This is familiar to anyone exploiting a production line for the purposes of manufacture. In the car industry, for example, it is defined by the frequency with which the product must be changed significantly enough to require "retooling" the assembly line.

In fact the pipeline is a very powerful model for both domain *and* function decomposition, or even a mixture of both. What renders it unique and so very efficient is the extremely simple *communication archi-*

tecture which defines it. Communication is synchronous and has a very simple protocol. It remains equally effective when extended to two (or more) dimensions to create what are called *systolic*[3], or "heartbeat", algorithms because information flows rhythmically in a preferred direction.

Note that there are two distinct interpretations of the pipeline, as applied to the construction (assembly) of a wall. A worker may be imagined passing to a successor a signal to access his layer in the wall. Alternatively, the worker may be imagined passing the wall itself, in its current state. In the case of wall construction it is clearly more practical for workers to move around to permit appropriate access to the wall than move the wall itself around. But in the case of gearbox assembly (construction) it is clearly easier to move the gearbox around and have the workers remain in place because a conveyor belt renders the necessary communication easier and more efficient.

The appropriate kind of communication will depend upon the particular application and forms a critical factor in system design, as Henry Ford demonstrated to such effect three-quarters of a century ago.

1.2.2 Alternation

We all know that nowadays, to our cost, our jobs require us to juggle multiple tasks. Our lives are just not as simple as those of our ancestors. As modern workers, we are expected to be able to *alternate* between multiple tasks. To do so requires a new skill known as "time management". Each time we change tasks we must *switch context* appropriately.

In order to learn how multiple tasks must be managed, consider the example of a person playing two distinct games of chess. The "multi-player" must respond to a move made by an opponent (Fig. 1.7). When one opponent makes a move the multi-player must forget all about the game played against the other and respond. The multi-player must recall the history and strategy adopted for the game in which the response is to be made.

Figure 1.7 Alternation between two games.

Each player must send a message containing a move made. The multi-player must respond with a message of the same type. The task of playing a game of chess is fundamentally the same for all three players. The multi-player may thus be said to be performing two instances of the same task.

An efficient algorithm for the multi-player is repeatedly to wait, idle, until an opponent makes a move. The multi-player then responds to that opponent. It makes no sense whatsoever to allow *interruption* of this response by the other opponent. Any move made by the other opponent has to await a response until that to the first is complete. By allowing the multi-player to suspend play after making a response to each move, rather than selfishly expecting him to wait around for the next one, each player is co-operating with the other. On the other hand, they are in competition for attention when they announce their move. Should they both announce a move simultaneously then the multi-player must find a way to resolve the contention.

The multi-player must *alternate* between games according to the attention demanded by each player. As well as resolving contention somehow, the multi-player may also be required to be *fair*. The term "fair" must then be carefully and precisely defined.

Efficient parallel organization requires a balance between co-operation and competition. The nature of that balance will be different according to the demands of each application. However, as was emphasized earlier, co-operation is by far the more important principle.

1.3 Competition

1.3.1 Time management

In the previous section the idea of a worker having to allocate time to multiple tasks was introduced and it was shown how this may imply alternating between them according to which was ready to proceed. If none are ready then the worker will be idle. The response to each message received was completed without interruption. This is an example of a local *scheduling algorithm.*

It was pointed out that each player allowed the multi-player to *suspend* playing a game and *resume* another, if possible. The multi-player was thus being co-operative. This way of sharing the resource of time is known as *co-operative multi-tasking*. It is very efficient but relies upon all tasks being co-operative and not selfishly hogging the worker's time.

Life becomes a lot more complicated when tasks differ, and they usually do differ in both size and importance. Anyone experienced (and effective) in managing their own time will know that these two attributes may be folded into one. Tasks on a "to-do" list can only be ranked in one dimension. Bigger tasks must be assigned a lower *priority* than those which are smaller, but of equal importance, because fewer of them may be completed in the same window of time. Each task must thus be assigned a priority which takes account of both its size and importance.

Co-operative multi-tasking may be refined to account for the differing priority of tasks by allowing the interruption of an active task, *but only by one of higher priority*. It is thus necessary to know from whence a message comes *before* reading its contents. Here we uncover a profound problem with the telephone which shows it to be quite unsuited to modern work. One has to answer the phone, receive the message, *and* respond to it, regardless of the task to which it relates. Modern work is very communication intensive. The phone rings frequently and commonly causes people to lose control of their time management. Yet one cannot dispense with a synchronous channel such as the phone. Some messages will relate to tasks of higher priority than the currently active one and thus warrant immediate response. Electronic mail offers an excellent alternative, provided it is used in conjunction with an interface capable of informing one when mail has arrived, and of offering one the chance to scan who it is from and what it is about. Sadly, after 30 years of "email" being technically possible there is still no sign of a standard and affordable system with universal access.

Tasks vary in the amount of communication they require. For those which are much less dependent upon communication, an alternative to co-operative multi-tasking exists. This time tasks need not be deliberately co-operative in the manner in which they are performed. A rigid schedule is adopted, where time is allocated to tasks according to their priority. Tasks are brutally interrupted regardless of their progress. Such a scheduling algorithm may be referred to as *competitive multi-tasking* since there is no requirement for tasks to be performed in a co-operative manner. Anyone attempting to manage their own time in this simple-minded way should not expect efficiency but, in jobs where communication matters, should instead expect to earn a reputation for being rather unresponsive and for suffering unwarranted stress!

1.3.2 Service provision

Competition for access to a worker's time is an example of something more general. The worker's time is a single resource which must be shared amongst tasks. In most human systems there are other *shared resources*.

Perhaps our most valuable shared resource is our food supply. When we go to a shop to retrieve some food we expect to be provided with *service*. The protocol for interaction with a service provider, like a shop, is another skill which we learn as children, and which we take for granted utterly. As a client, we make our *request* to the server, who then (usually) *grants* it. This is a *client/server* protocol which will also incorporate rules for the particular *transaction* requested, such as how much money must pass to the server to retrieve a quantity of the requested item.

Any effective client/server protocol must also provide rules to govern the behaviour to be expected when multiple clients wish to make requests of a single server. Those rules must be fair, by which we mean that *all clients are equally likely to receive service.* Perhaps the most common such protocol is that of the *queue.* The great disadvantage with the queue is that clients are *busy waiting.* A common, but expensive, response to this problem is to exploit domain decomposition and replicate servers, resulting in multiple shorter queues.

Nowadays, we tend to use the same shop to make many different purchases. It is entirely up to us, while we are in the shop, how we schedule those tasks. However, that is not possible when we leave. There is only one task left to perform, that of paying, which must be completed before we can begin any other. Multiple, identical servers and queues offer the only solution, which is usually cost effective since they serve the entire supermarket. It is not likely to be cost effective for each counter *within* the supermarket.

Within the supermarket it is instead possible to exploit the fact that clients are multi-tasking. If one counter is busy then a client can suspend that task and resume another. It only remains for the server on each counter to provide a mechanism by which the server may inform clients that it is ready to serve them. A very simple solution, called the *ticket algorithm,* may be found in almost any modern, efficient supermarket. The client collects a numbered ticket from the server. Each time the server completes a transaction the number is incremented and displayed around the shop. A bell may be sounded to signal that the number has changed. Client and server may thus synchronize their transaction.

Use of the ticket algorithm is only worthwhile where service takes significant time (e.g. the cheese counter) and queues otherwise build up. As before, with allocating workers' time, life gets a lot more difficult, and a successful algorithm more complicated, when clients have varying priority. This is why most common service providers limit priority to a simple binary divide ("high" and "low") and simply provide a duplicate server for each.

The existence of the ticket algorithm obviates any need to queue when one might do something else. It could undoubtedly be exploited much more widely than it is currently, particularly in airports and railway stations where clients might spend less time queuing and more time relaxing comfortably while awaiting service. The art of designing service provision would seem to be that of *reducing communication to that inherent in the problem*[4].

1 Sadly, as a species, we are not alone in perpetrating organized violence. Chimpanzees have been observed to make war as well.

2 The evolution of speech must be an enormous survival advantage to counteract the inherent disadvantage. Humans are the only creatures able to choke to death, an ability which results from the same physical change which allows us to speak. Attempting to speak and eat at the same time causes death frequently and is thus one kind of parallel processing not recommended.

3 Usually means "rhythmically pumped", like as by a heart. Derived from the Ancient Greek word *systole* which means contraction.

4 A wonderful example is the service offered by the shop from which the author purchases pet supplies. A phone call enables the request (placing the order) and the grant of service (including the day on which the supplies will be delivered). The transaction is completed by leaving a cheque stuck to the front door which is exchanged for the supplies. That shop does good business, even in hard times.

Chapter 2

The Nature of Parallel Systems

2.1 Abstraction

2.1.1 Processor, process, and procedure

A processor may be thought of as the analogue of a human worker and a process as that of a task. Just as a worker performs a task, so a processor runs a process.

Workers must somehow know which tasks to perform. A supervisor must allocate tasks to each worker. In just the same way, processes must be allocated to processors, either statically or dynamically. If multiple processes are allocated to a processor then it must itself allocate time to each according to some built-in scheduling algorithm.

Figure 2.1 Processor, process, and procedure abstractions.

Workers must also know how to perform each task. Just as they must be trained to perform their tasks so processors require access to the appropriate procedure for each process allocated, which describes the sequence of actions of which it is composed (Fig. 2.1).

2.1.2 Link, channel, and protocol

A channel is a communication path between a pair of processes. Just as a processor is the physical mechanism on which a process runs, a link is the physical mechanism which supports a channel (Fig. 2.2). A link may transport something physical which contains information, such as a person or a floppy disk, or it may transport the information itself directly (e.g. a telephone or LAN connection).

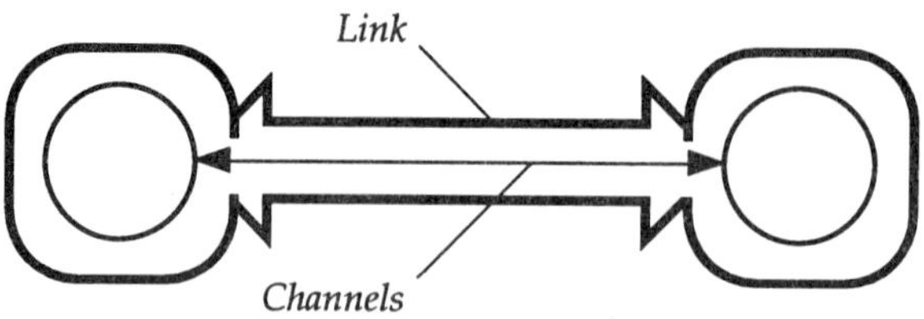

Figure 2.2 Link and channel abstractions.

Before communication can proceed on any given channel, a protocol must be agreed by the processes which share it. A protocol is a set of rules which govern the use of a channel. A channel may thus be thought of as a link plus a protocol.

The concept of protocol originated with diplomacy. Before two heads of state may meet, a number of conditions must be satisfied. It is usually possible to layer such protocols so that the conditions depend upon each other in a hierarchical fashion. The same is true of digital systems. Lower conditions are satisfied by hardware mechanisms and higher ones by software.

The protocol of a channel for communication between two software processes must include everything which dictates how it may be used. The programming environment should hide as many of the gory details as possible, leaving the programmer free to be concerned only with the when and what of the communication inherent in the algorithm employed.

2.2 Performance

2.2.1 Requirement

Specifying precisely what one means by performance is not as simple as it might first seem. It depends upon the requirements of the application concerned. If the application is one of data processing then the most sensible performance measure is that of *data throughput*, in other words, the number of atomic data elements processed per unit time. In the case of wall construction this corresponds to the number of bricks laid per hour (day, or whatever). Similarly, in a graphics rendering application our concern might be the number of pixels illuminated correctly per second.

The other possibility of interest is that of *responsiveness*, by which we mean the expected value of the delay between an event occurring and the response of the system to it. Many applications now require embedded systems, where the computer is embedded within a larger system. Their purpose is usually to generate real-time response to events which occur, within either the larger system, or its environment. The meaning of "real time" is somewhat vague but may be taken to imply that an event meets a response before the next one occurs. It may also be applied to data processing where it implies that data are processed as they are generated, element by element. An example of a real-time embedded system is a computer which controls the flight of an aircraft. The pilot no longer directly controls the flight but instead issues requests to the computer which decides whether, and if so, how best, to obey. The computer must respond; in real time, both to changes in the aircraft attitude and to the pilot moving the control column.

A third performance measure is only really useful for commercial advertisement and has little or no technical value. *Instruction throughput* refers to the number of atomic machine instructions executed per second. This is meaningless unless one states precisely which instructions are concerned. It may be that a million integer additions can be executed per second but many other operations are required to execute an entire program. The speed of comparisons, branching, procedure invocation, and file access must also be considered. Surprising results are frequently encountered when the manufacturers' statistics are set aside and the speeds measured with which a single useful task may be performed. The ranking thus arrived at will doubtless change when a different task is used for comparison.

The actual requirement will be some combination of data throughput and responsiveness according to the target application.

2.2.2 Efficiency

The whole point of parallel processing is to complete a task more quickly by employing multiple workers. It is thus of interest to know the factor by which the time taken for completion has been reduced. This is known as the *speedup*.

$$S_n = t_1/t_n$$

Note that it does not matter how we define performance. t may refer to the time taken to process an atomic data element *or* the expected (average) time taken to respond to an event *or* to some weighted combination thereof. t_n refers to the time taken with n processors and should always be less than t_1.

Processors, like workers, cost money. It is clearly important that full utilization of the processing resource purchased is achieved. Linear speedup refers to the increase of performance in direct proportion to the number of processors employed. It is thus possible to define *efficiency* as the speedup per processor.

$$E_n = \frac{S_n}{n} = \frac{t_1}{n.t_n}$$

Efficiency will therefore be unity when a workforce of size n gets the job done n times more quickly. If it is any slower then efficiency will be less in direct proportion.

As we discovered in the previous chapter, sharing a workload demands co-operation which in turn demands communication. It is sometimes written that communication in a parallel computer is an overhead. This is nonsense. Communication *not inherent in the problem* is an overhead. (An example of communication which *is* an overhead is that required to implement dynamic process allocation.) The art of parallel algorithm design is to reduce the communication to no more than that which is essential.

Any processor designed to form part of a parallel computer must support communication, i.e. it must sport links. Efficiency demands full utilization of *all* physical resources, processing, *and* communication. The problem we face is therefore that of determining the processing and communication which must be carried out and that of achieving a match with the processing and communication resources available. This is a key problem in the design of parallel software to which we shall return in Chapter 5.

2.2.3 Scalability

Scalability refers to the ability to retain efficiency as the size of the workforce increases, in other words to the constant form of E as a function of n over some given regime.

$$E(n) \to const \qquad (n_1 < n < n_2)$$

Note that $E(1)$ is always unity. Very often the regime of interest begins with $n = 1$. Our concern then is just how many processors can we employ before our software becomes unacceptably inefficient. Figure 2.3 depicts the typical variation of E with n, exaggerated a little for clarity.

Scalability is the "holy grail" of parallel computing. Its achievement implies that performance may be balanced against cost and demand. For example, given a scalable system, a researcher acquiring a new grant can add performance by adding to the previously available computing resource. It is not necessary to throw existing equipment away and buy new to attain increased performance. If the new kit is twice as fast as the old then a three-fold improvement is possible instead of a mere doubling. A far greater impact is that upon commercial products which depend upon computational performance, of which there are now many. A cheaper product may be obtained which incorporates no more processing power than necessary. A more competitive product may be obtained where performance can be scaled as required and traded against cost, without the need for expensive and risky software redesign and recomposition.

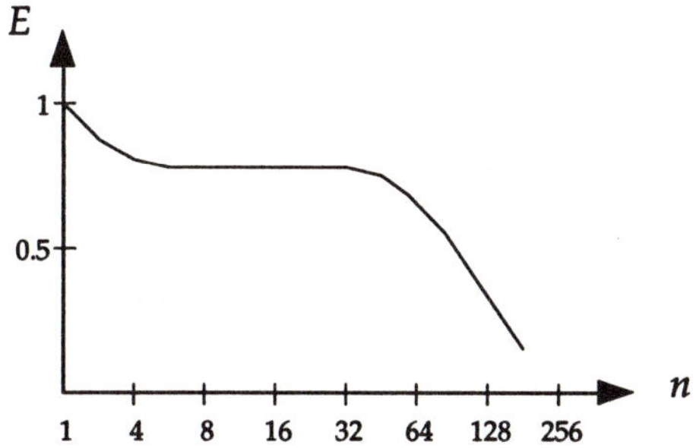

Figure 2.3 Scalability from about four to about 32 processors.

There is one prime reason why scalability is difficult to achieve in practice. As the domain grows the communication *requirement* will grow in a way which depends upon the algorithm. As the number of processors grows the communication *resource* will grow in a way which depends upon the way in which processors are interconnected. The problem of balancing requirement and resource which we faced earlier to maximize efficiency is now compounded if we are to achieve scalability too. Again, we shall return later to this topic.

2.3 Communication

2.3.1 Synchronous communication

If we are to understand parallel systems then we must understand communication. *All* human organization is parallel. It is in fact already the case that almost all computers are in some way parallel. It simply remains possible *so far* to hide that fact from programmers. It will not remain so much longer. Programmers too therefore need to understand communication in order to allow explicit parallel programming.

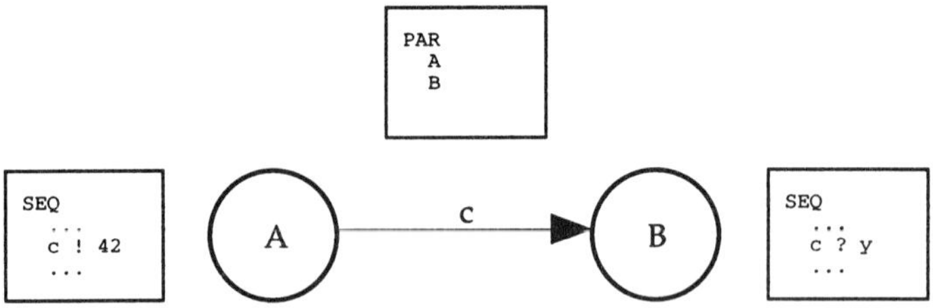

Figure 2.4 Synchronous communication.

Suppose two processes, *A* and *B*, are to communicate over some shared channel *c*, and further that *A* is ready to send a message before *B* is ready to receive it (Fig.2.4). If *A* must *wait* for *B* then communication is said to be *synchronous* because a common point in time may be thus identified for both *A* and *B*. The two processes must synchronize for the message transfer. Note that there is no possibility of *data loss* in synchronous communication.

Time points may be enumerated, for any process, which correspond to *events* which each fall into one of two categories, communication (message transfer) or state update[1]. A list of such events, composed as they are observed, is called a *trace*. Note that a communication event is shared between communicating processes at the moment of synchronization. It is in fact merely the update of state across a domain boundary.

2.3.2 Asynchronous communication

If the same two processes are considered again, but with the single distinction that *A* does *not* have to wait for *B* before sending the message, then communication is said to be asynchronous. It is no longer possible to identify a common point in time between the two processes.

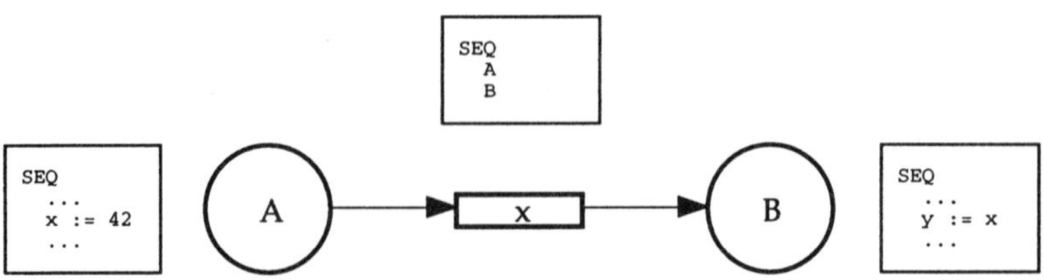

Figure 2.5 Asynchronous communication.

With asynchronous communication the message itself has to wait for *B*. The place where it waits is called a *buffer*. We can see from Figure 2.5 that asynchronous communication and traditional, purely sequential, programming are one and the same thing, where the buffers employed are just the variables declared.

Note also that *B* must *not* become ready to receive before *A*. If it does so then communication will fail because *B* has no way of knowing when *A* is ready. Similarly *A* has no way of knowing when *B* becomes ready. Hence *A* may easily overwrite data which have not yet been read.

➤ Asynchronous communication between concurrent processes allows the possibility of data loss.

The system depicted in Figure 2.5 renders it certain that this cannot occur by insisting that *B* cannot start until *A* has terminated. Should a mechanism be provided to allow *B* to know when *A* becomes ready, and it is appropriately used, then communication will, in fact, become synchronous. That mechanism effects synchronization and thus forms a channel.

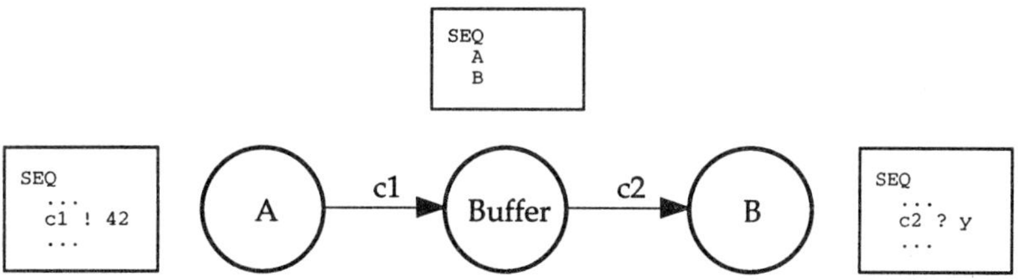

Figure 2.6 Asynchronous communication from synchronous channels.

Synchronous communication is more fundamental than the asynchronous kind. If all we have available are asynchronous channels then we can *never* communicate synchronously. However, if we have synchronous channels then we can easily communicate asynchronously, merely by introducing a *buffer process* as intermediary. In the system shown in Figure 2.6, *A* is able to proceed immediately after message transmission and the buffer process does the waiting. What if *A* transmits another message before *B* accepts the first? A simple solution is just to replicate the buffer process, making as many copies as is necessary, assuming one knows *in advance* how many that is.

2.3.3 Synchronization

In the last chapter we discovered that the most basic requirement of co-operation is the ability to synchronize actions. We went on to discover just how useful it is to pass messages when it occurs, but the fundamentally important requirement remains synchronization itself. How is it achieved? There are three basic methods.

First, we shall discuss the method most commonly employed by humans, which will explain the popularity among us of, if not downright dependency upon, personal time-pieces (watches). Synchronization in the workplace is mostly achieved by reference to a *common clock*. Meetings are scheduled via this mechanism. What is a meeting if not synchronized communication between a number of workers? Computers too are heavily dependent upon this method. All conventional digital systems, such as processors, are synchronous systems where synchronization is achieved via a common clock[2]. Apart from the need for universal access, a common clock has another disadvantage. It creates arbitrary constraints upon process scheduling and message transfer. Synchronization either has to occur at regular intervals, whether or not it is required (e.g. operation of a synchronous digital system), or has to be somehow primed in advance (e.g. scheduling a meeting).

A common alternative is *handshaking*. The first process ready to communicate, in either direction, asserts a signal and awaits another one from the second. It is said to be "busy waiting" since it cannot suspend to allow the processor to resume another process.

Rendezvous is the way both occam™ and Ada solve the problem. Rendezvous in a computer is conducted in exactly the same way as two humans would. First, a rendezvous location must be agreed. Let us say a couple agree to meet under the clock tower at Waterloo Station in London. Suppose the man arrives first to find no partner waiting. Instead of hanging around, bored and idle, he leaves a note on the wall to indicate that he may be found in a particular pub. As long as he leaves the note he is free to occupy himself as he chooses. When his partner arrives, she need only follow the pointer to complete the rendezvous. It does not matter who arrives first, it will still work.

Two processes rendezvous in a computer in much the same way. A rendezvous location must be agreed as part of the channel protocol[3]. It need only be a location in memory but it must be initialized empty by storing therein a preferred value. This is enough to indicate to the first process ready to communicate that its partner is not yet ready. It stores a pointer to itself in the rendezvous location and then suspends, freeing the processor to resume another process, if possible. The partner process is thus able to know that it is second to arrive and also to complete the transfer by following the pointer. Either process may be ready first. (The system is symmetric.) Neither need keep its processor busy waiting.

2.4 Behaviour

2.4.1 Process allocation and scheduling

As we have previously concluded, processes must be allocated to processors, either *statically* (once, before work commences) or *dynamically* (repeatedly, as work proceeds). Each individual processor must be capable of scheduling processes, in order not to be idle while a process awaits synchronization.

Allocation and scheduling should be thought of as the scheduling of processes in *time* and *space* respectively. One should imagine a two-dimensional surface with time enumerated along one axis and processor identity along the other. The job of allocating processes along the processor axis may be referred to as global scheduling and that along the time axis as local scheduling.

Local scheduling requires that each processor be able to suspend a running process and resume a ready process. There are thus three possible *process states*: ready, running, and suspended (waiting). Figure 2.7 shows the allowed process state transitions. There can only ever be a single process in the running state on each processor. Whenever the running process changes the processor must switch all memory that forms the context of processing. The speed with which a *context switch* may be carried out is an important characteristic of the processor which will affect the granularity of software design. The more rapid the context switch, the more frequently processes may be suspended and resumed, the finer the grain of process which may be scheduled.

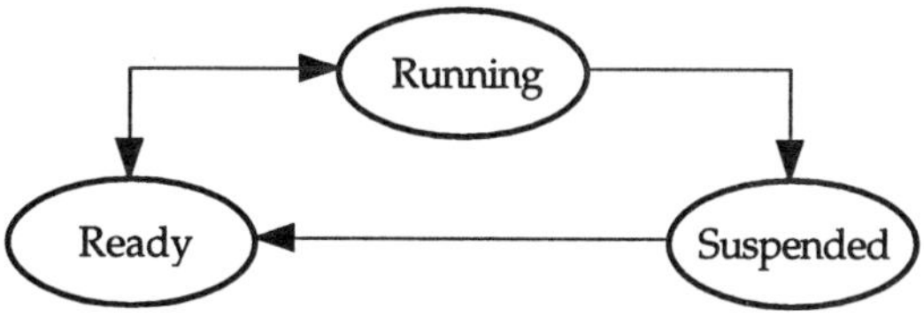

Figure 2.7 Process state transitions.

Ready processes are held in a *ready queue* which is accessible to the scheduler (sometimes called a "supervisor"). Where processes possess a priority attribute a priority queue must be used. Typically, a process may only be *pre-empted*, and thus moved back to the ready queue, by one of higher priority. Where all processes possess the same priority, or where no priority attribute exists, the scheduling algorithm will need periodically to swap processes from ready to running. The need for such "time-slicing" is greatly reduced, however, if the processes concerned co-operate effectively. Any scheduling algorithm is thus a mixture of co-operation and competition.

2.4.2 Communication infrastructure

We have seen just how important communication is to parallel organization. The structure of any parallel system is basically that of the communication involved. We shall see later on that an effective way to design and implement a parallel system is to construct and test a communication infrastructure first, and later add function. There are three fundamental kinds of infrastructure possible.

Local communication is that which takes place only within the process neighbourhood. No such message need traverse more than one channel. A consequence of this class of communication is that it scales linearly with the number of processes. This means that it requires a communication resource which is *constant* per processor. Processors may therefore be identical in this respect, and thus potentially manufactured more cheaply.

Global communication is that which may occur between any pair of processes in a network. Messages must thus be forwarded over an output channel chosen according to a *routing algorithm* which depends upon the network topology. They may travel a distance whose maximum equals the diameter of the network. Processing must then be committed to message routing and forwarding at each node of the network. This represents an overhead which makes global communication relatively expensive. Another disadvantage is its scaling property. As the network grows so does its diameter, which means that each message requires correspondingly more processing (routing) and more communication resources. The quantity of messages per processor (node) may remain constant as the network grows but the expense of transporting them per processor grows.

Special communication is that which may occur between any process and one which is special, usually a service provider or farmer. Message routing and forwarding is required and becomes *concentrated*, near the special process, giving rise to a *bottleneck* effect. The only solution to such a bottleneck is to delegate. In the case of service provision it is necessary to distribute the service provided across the process network.

2.4.3 Pathological behaviour

Pathological behaviour results from the failure to co-operate. There are as many forms as there are ways to fail. Whatever the cause, the symptoms are usually obvious and the results catastrophic. Note, however, that the symptoms of the *possibility* of pathological behaviour may *not* be obvious. No system can be labelled secure if such behaviour is possible. No system is safe if it is not secure[4]. Many modern computer applications are safety critical.

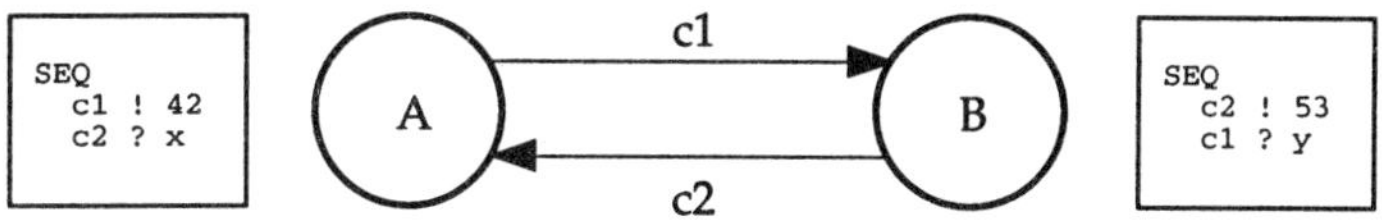

Figure 2.8 Deadlock.

Deadlock is said to have occurred when no process in a given network is able to proceed. It is caused by a *cycle of dependency* where each process waits for ever to communicate with its successor. To render a system secure against deadlock it is necessary to guarantee that it can *never* occur. In a system of co-operating processes there can be no recovery from deadlock once it occurs. In Figure 2.8 *A* and *B* run in parallel but cannot agree on how to interact initially. They will therefore both remain inert for ever.

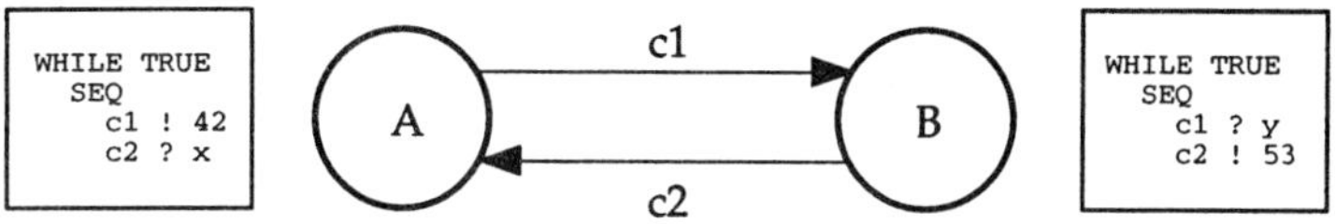

Figure 2.9 Livelock.

Livelock is said to have occurred when processes are locked in a "deadly embrace" of repeated communication and are thus unable to communicate externally. To all other processes of the system, or to the environment, it is as though they have terminated. In one regard livelock is worse than deadlock. The processes concerned are live and thus are using up the processing resource. Otherwise the symptoms will appear the same as for deadlock. Figure 2.9 shows a livelocked system. The combination of *A* and *B* repeats the same cycle of interaction for ever. It is easy to contrive an example of such behaviour but to *prove* that any given system of interest will *never* exhibit it is a different matter entirely. It is unfortunately beyond the scope of this book.

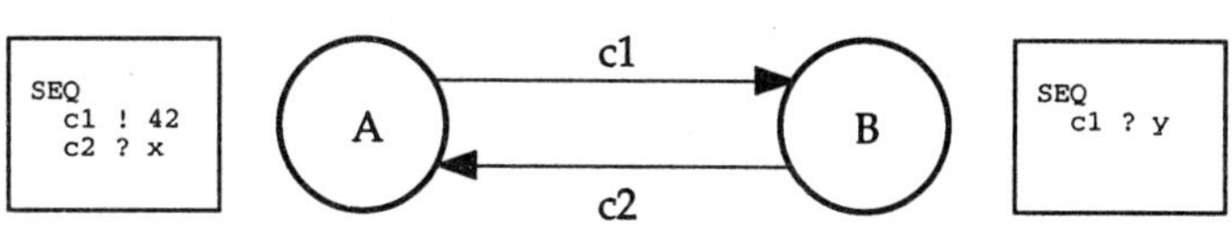

Figure 2.10 Starvation.

Starvation of a process is said to occur if any attempt at communication remains unsatisfied. All processes which are party to deadlock suffer starvation as do any which try to communicate with another which is party to livelock. Figure 2.10 shows a system where one process terminates without satisfying a requirement of its partner for interaction. *A* starves because *B* terminated prematurely.

1 Any reader familiar with the ideas of object-oriented programming will recognize message transfer and state update as characterizing an instance of a class of object as it runs. Processes may be thought of as a *run-time* unit of software, the counterpart of a module which is a unit of source code. It is important to be aware that run-time and source modularity are distinct and will differ.

2 The distribution of a common clock becomes *much* more difficult when the tick frequency rises towards the limit set by the technology employed. *Asynchronous* digital systems are currently the subject of academic research and seem to offer great promise.

3 In fact, an occam channel name is *bound* to its associated rendezvous location.

4 Safety may be quantified as the *product* of the probability of failure and a measure of the consequences of failure. This is why airliners and nuclear reactors are so difficult to render acceptably safe. The consequences of failure are so appalling that the probability has to be so low that it is all but impossible to measure adequately.

Chapter 3

Programming Parallel Systems

3.1 Threads of control

3.1.1 Primitive of operation

Before we can even begin to discuss how a parallel computer might be programmed, it is necessary to reconsider the precise nature of the machine whose behaviour we seek to control.

There is so very much variation in how interprocess co-operation is achieved that, at present, there is almost no portability of parallel software whatsoever. It is therefore quite impossible yet to answer the question of how parallel systems may be programmed in general. However, there are some features which remain present in all architectures which help at least to understand the problem.

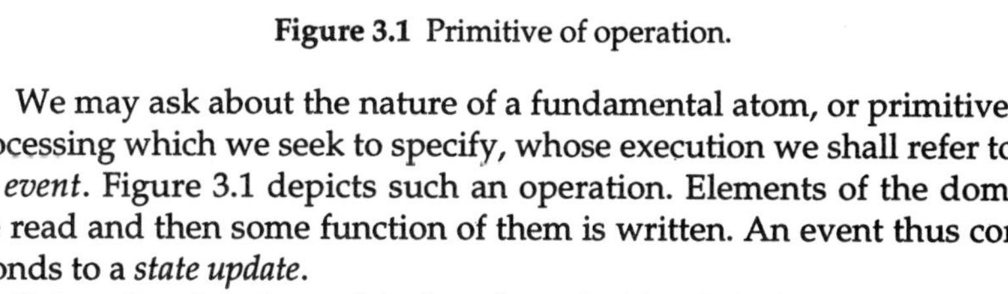

Figure 3.1 Primitive of operation.

We may ask about the nature of a fundamental atom, or primitive, of processing which we seek to specify, whose execution we shall refer to as an *event*. Figure 3.1 depicts such an operation. Elements of the domain are read and then some function of them is written. An event thus corresponds to a *state update*.

It is quite clear from this that the primitive is in fact *communication* and *transformation*. Because we are usually most familiar with the procedure programming abstraction, we may immediately associate an event with the execution of an assignment statement. All forms of abstraction require the naming of objects which may then be inter-related to form a model. Here it is state (a cell within the domain) which is named, as are procedures, which are then associated with the state required for their completion and with each other in the hierarchy required for the completion of the overall task.

Assignment is really just a direct assertion of the primitive rather than an interpretation. The procedure is said to be a very low-level abstraction because it remains very close to that of the machine itself. An alternative is *function evaluation*. The state written is interpreted as the value of the function and that read as its arguments. This time there is no need explicitly to name state.

An important generalization of the primitive is that it might affect multiple data. That discussed above takes *vector*[1] input to produce *scalar* output. In general, however, there is no reason why a single indivisible operation should not take multiple vector input and produce vector output. In a way, all conventional computers perform vector computation when they add two integers. Each bit of the output is effectively generated simultaneously. Such a machine is said to be "bit-parallel". For numerical computation, word-parallel machines are common. For example, such machines can compute the product of two matrices in a single operation. A single primitive (machine-code instruction) is all that is required to cause this to happen.

3.1.2 Thread and domain

There now remains the problem of how to specify the *event ordering*, or indeed whether to do so *explicitly* at all. It should be born in mind that a program is a statement of *intended* behaviour. On the other hand, a *trace* lists events in the order in which they were *observed* actually to occur.

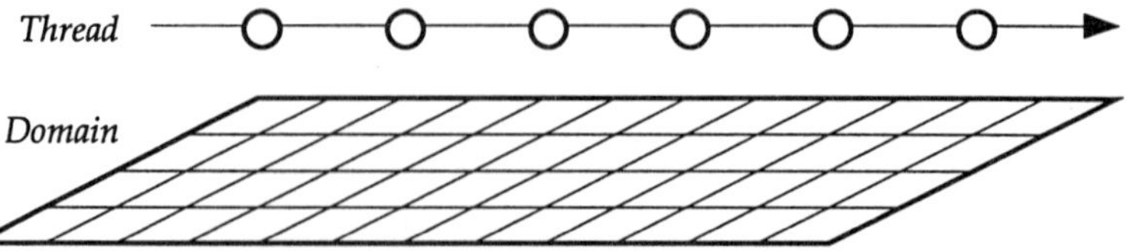

Figure 3.2 Thread of control and its domain.

It is always helpful to have a visualization of any abstract model which is the subject of reasoning. Our model (Fig. 3.2) is principally that of a domain whose state is updated sequentially. Just one event may take place at a time and may be thought of as a tick of an abstract clock. It thus proves useful to imagine the event ordering as the threading of beads. It is obviously impossible to have two beads occupying the same position. The nature and order of the beads dictate behaviour and the eventual state of the entire domain on which they act. Domain and thread are bound together. The domain of any thread may be defined as the union of just that state which is acted upon by any bead upon that thread. Each single *thread of control* may be regarded as the trace of a process.

Explicit specification of the order in which events occur is known as *imperative* programming. The alternative, known as *declarative* programming, merely specifies the effect the thread is to have upon its domain, leaving some automation (at either run-time or compile-time) to determine ordering.

3.1.3 Forking and joining

Processes are never completely independent of one another if they are co-operating. However, the possibility exists for threads to be considered independent over a given interval. Consider the program fragment in Listing 3.1.

```
SEQ
  A
  PAR
    B
    C
  D
```

Listing 3.1 Programmed fork and join.

The program listed dictates constraints upon the order in which events may occur. No event of *B* or *C* may occur until *A* has terminated. Similarly, no event in *D* may occur until both *B* and *C* have terminated. To learn more about the events themselves, and further constraints upon their order, some description of the processes *A* to *D* must be sought. Figure 3.3 shows how the ideas of thread and process are related.

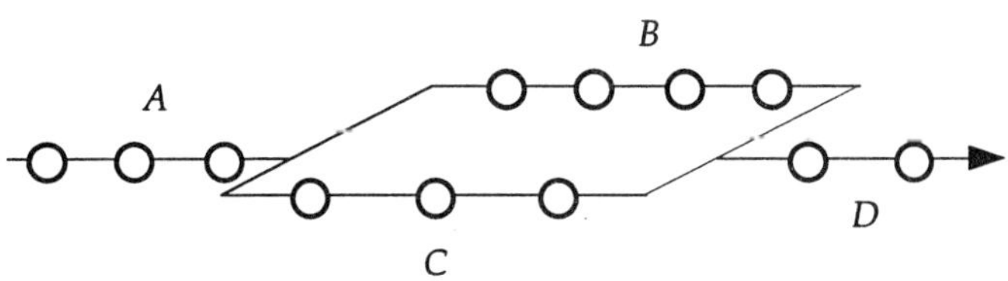

Figure 3.3 Forking and joining of thread of control.

A *fork* in a control thread specifies the possibility that two or more events may follow the one which precedes the fork, in any order. They may even occur simultaneously. A *join* specifies that before the following event may occur those which precede it must have already occurred. Therefore a join infers a point at which *synchronization* occurs. Figure 3.3 shows the fork from *A* into *B* and *C*, followed by the join of *B* and *C* prior to the start of *D*. One may prefer to think of two threads that exist for the duration of all four processes. *A* and *D* therefore run along both threads. Alternatively, one might prefer to think of all processes running along a single thread which splits at a fork and which merges into other threads at a join. Either view is valid but the second is more consistent with existing terminology and a little more flexible.

Figure 3.3 merely shows an example of the flow of control which we may wish to specify. It is just as likely that multiple control threads may be required which first join and *then* fork.

We have said nothing about the domains of processes *A*, *B*, *C*, and *D* yet. To ask whether or how they interact is to ask how the processes communicate. That is the subject of the next section.

3.2 Communication

3.2.1 Distributed domain

Let us consider a design where domain decomposition has been performed so that there exists a unique process for each sub-domain. How do neighbouring processes communicate?

Interaction between neighbours occurs when the update of state within the domain of one depends upon state within the other. This situation is completely catered for by allowing the update of state in one to the value of a function whose arguments belong in the other. Such an event is much better described by a picture (Fig. 3.4).

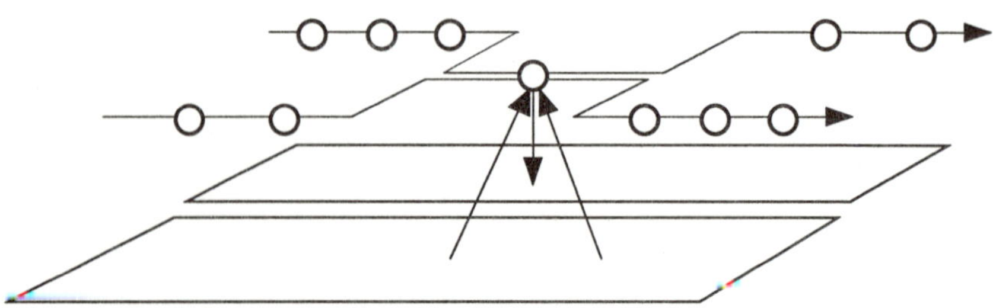

Figure 3.4 Synchronous communication across distributed domains.

We can see that this may be accomplished by threading *one bead on both threads*. Communication is clearly synchronous since neither process may proceed until it has been completed. Each process requires distinct programming; hence *output* is programmed in one and *input* in the other. The two halves of a single bead join over both threads. Note, however, that it is a *single* bead, indivisible along the thread direction. It still represents a single state update.

The joining of threads represents their points of synchronization, where messages may be passed. In an earlier chapter we encountered the requirement that any parallel algorithm must only include the minimum necessary communication. This style of parallel programming achieves just that. Threads begin separately and are completely independent *except* where synchronization occurs.

3.2.2 Shared domain

The whole idea here is that a number of distinct processes are to process the same domain as independently as possible. Those occasions when state is updated by one process to be later read by another is regarded as communication. The question we are truly asking therefore is how we may render such communication *secure*. This reduces to the following requirements.

- To ensure that only one process at a time may write each cell in the domain.
- To ensure that any shared cell is not read until it has been written.
- To ensure that any shared cell is not rewritten until it has first been read.

When two processes are to communicate via shared domain one must write in the cell which the other must later read. The cell must not be overwritten until it has first been read. This implies synchronization. A little thought will quickly reveal that the only way that this may be achieved is by means of a reserved cell in the shared domain which must be initialized to a value which indicates to a process that it is the first to arrive at the *critical section* of its thread where communication is to occur. It is also clear that critical sections must be preceded by a fork so that initialization may occur. Shared domain parallel programming is thus of the style where forks precede joins, the reverse of that applicable to distributed domain programming (Fig. 3.5).

Wherever distinct threads share common domain it is clearly possible that simultaneous attempts might be made to update a cell within that domain. Clearly no sane programmer should allow this possibility since effort would be expended without determinable result. All shared domain should be protected by *mutual exclusion* of access, by which we mean that, at any given time, only one process should have access to each cell. Mutual exclusion of domain access is guaranteed by mutual exclusion of entry to critical sections which access shared domain if all such domain is regarded as the means of interprocess communication. Note, however, that there need be *no* mutual exclusion protecting any domain against multiple *read* access.

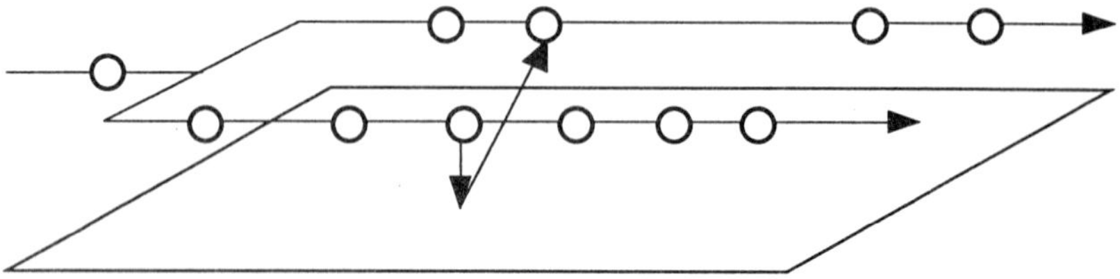

Figure 3.5 Asynchronous communication within shared domain.

It is a simplification to assume that cells may be updated simultaneously by distinct processes. In a conventional (so-called "von-Neumann") architecture only one access at a time is possible over the entire domain.

Shared domain systems are the result of functional decomposition. The great disadvantage of such an approach is that programming access to the shared domain leaves program security firmly at the lowest level of system construction, i.e. in the lap of the programmer. In any branch of engineering some responsibility devolves to those who conduct implementation. A missing rivet in a bridge could cause it to collapse but good design renders this unlikely. Unfortunately, it is still the case when engineering software that the equivalent of the missing rivet *will* be catastrophic, perhaps even fatal. Secure parallel software is very much easier to achieve via domain decomposition and programming synchronous communication between distributed domains.

3.2.3 Interchanging variable and channel

Synchronous communication over a channel results in precisely the same update of state as does an assignment. The single difference is that it provides a mechanism for the assigned value to be a function of state within another domain. Should both source and destination state exist within the same domain then a straightforward assignment may be used instead. This equivalence represents an example of a *law of programming* which infers a *program transform* which may be employed to change the way in which a program is executed *without changing its meaning* with regard to state update.

Listing 3.2 shows how a variable, used for asynchronous communication, may be interchanged with a channel, used for synchronous communication. Note how a buffer variable (x) has been introduced for asynchronous communication. A further transformation is now obvious. We could dispense with x and merge the two SEQ processes into one and conduct the communication as a single assignment. Note also the symmetry between the way in which variables are declared over a SEQ and channels over a PAR. This is how it should be.

```
REAL32 x :
SEQ
  SEQ
    ...
    x := 0.5*g*(t^2)
    ...
  SEQ
    ...
    y := x
    ...
```

≡

```
CHAN OF REAL32 c :
PAR
  SEQ
    ...
    c ! 0.5*g*(t^2)
    ...
  SEQ
    ...
    c ? y
    ...
```

Listing 3.2 Interchanging a variable for a channel.

This is a very useful way to transform programs for the following reason, to which we shall return later. Although most people still learn to program in a purely sequential fashion and without the benefit of synchronous communication, it is nonetheless true that the most natural algorithms are parallel. The way to design parallel software is to begin with the most parallel algorithm possible and then gradually render it more sequential by means of the above transformation until it suits the machine on which it is to run[2]. In other words, the *granularity* is recursively decreased to match that of the target machine.

3.2.4 Increasing the scope of PAR

There are other program transforms which result from the theory of Communicating Sequential Processes, and which help to obtain efficiency without affecting program meaning. One of the most useful allows the scope of PAR to be increased.

Suppose we manage to derive an algorithm of the form shown on the left hand side of Listing 3.3. This requires a fork into two processes *B* and *C* after the termination of *A*. A corresponding join is required after *B* and *C* terminate and before *D* can start. *A* and *B* communicate asynchronously via *v1*, as do C and *D* via *v2*. Finally, *B* and C communicate synchronously over channel *c*.

```
SEQ                                 PAR
  A(v1)                               SEQ
  PAR                                   A(v1)
    B(v1,c)                             B(v1,c)
    C(v2,c)           ≡               SEQ
  D(v2)                                 C(v2,c)
                                        D(v2)
```

Listing 3.3 Increasing the scope of PAR.

The only way we could run this algorithm and make use of two processors is if we allocate *A*, *B* (or *C*), and *D* to the first, and *C* (or *B*) to the second. This allows the second processor to be initially idle, waiting for *A* to terminate, and finally idle, while *D* runs. Also, we have to find some way for it to know when *C* may start. Clearly, this is not satisfactory.

If we had originally performed domain decomposition we would have noticed that *A* and *B* share some common domain, as do *C* and *D*, but there is no other sharing necessary. Hence it is possible to run these two pairs in parallel with each other.

The consequence of this transformation is that we may start two distinct control threads which need only touch (synchronize) at any point where the channel *c* is used. This suits true parallel processing (with multiple processors) much better, being much more efficient and easier to implement.

3.3 Programming metaphor

3.3.1 Procedure versus function

Programming means determining the behaviour of a machine. A program is a statement to that effect. In order to make such a statement, and thus correctly convey the intended meaning, a programming language is required. The syntax of such a language must guarantee a *unique* meaning of every possible statement, in order not to compromise program security. It must also fulfil two other aims.

First, the meaning of every program must not only describe a *valid* behaviour of the machine concerned but also describe an *efficient* behaviour. A program is meaningless as a pure abstraction. In the real world it is always a real, physical machine that is being programmed, with all its inherent physical characteristics, such as the consumption of energy and time.

Second, the composition must also be in terms of a human abstraction of what it is that the machine concerned actually does. This requirement perhaps explains the popularity of COBOL as a programming language for business applications, whereas it earned very little interest from scientists. Indeed, if a computer is used to implement the manufacture of fruit puddings then an ideal programming language will be one which features suitable terms. Operators should perhaps include `mix` and `bake`, and a `fruit` data type would undoubtedly be useful. Given that special purpose computer *hardware* has been developed quite often, it is perhaps surprising that more programming languages dedicated to a specific application area have not arisen, though there have been some[3].

Programming languages which describe behaviour purely in terms of what the machine actually does, rather than the application to which that machine is put, are referred to as *low-level* languages. There are two possible abstractions of the low-level operation of a computer (Fig. 3.1). A single (atomic) state update may be viewed as an action which assigns state, or as an evaluation of a *function*. In a program, action primitives are combined to form a *procedure*, and procedures combined to form larger procedures. The entire program is a statement of the "outermost" procedure together with those on which it depends, and so on. It reads as a list of commands and thus earns the label *imperative* programming. In the functional approach, primitive functions are evaluated, which allows the evaluation of abstract functions whose values may then form arguments to more abstract functions. The entire program is the declaration of such abstract functions and thus earns the label *declarative* programming.

Looking at a program as a pattern of data transformations to see how data flow it becomes clear that communication within a procedural program is basically *asynchronous* with variables serving as buffers. This is in contrast with a functional program, where no function may proceed until it has received the values of all its arguments and thus must employ *synchronous* communication. Another difference between the two programming metaphors is that procedural programming requires the *explicit* representation of the domain, whereas in a functional program it is *implicit*.

Functional programming has been around for a long time and has been the darling of many mathematically oriented academic computer scientists. It frees the programmer from the need to represent state explicitly and renders parallelism implicit. Why then has it failed to find much favour in commerce and industry? It might be that it simply fails to provide a match to the way in which most of us decompose problems. We just do not model the world as a hierarchy of functions evaluating themselves. Procedure abstraction, on the other hand, does offer such a match, *but only for problems of limited scale.* To use a manufacturing analogy, it is fairly easy to express how a gearbox is assembled via a procedure. It is not much more difficult to so describe how to keep a production line automatically fed with components. Try using procedure abstraction alone to express how an entire production plant operates and you may understand why something more is now called for.

3.3.2 Control versus data flow

Some of the advantages of functional programming were mentioned in the last section. It obviates the need to represent state explicitly and renders parallelism implicit. In addition, it also obviates the need for the programmer to render explicit the *control flow* within the program (which implies the order of beads upon the thread of control). Both the control flow and the communication required are inferred by the *data dependencies* rendered explicit in the program.

Computation can be viewed, at any level, as communication. In a functional program communication is synchronous, which means we can view any functional program as a particular *data flow* between input and output via various transformations specified as functions. The control flow is implicit in the program and must be derived by the compiler and/or some run-time operating system.

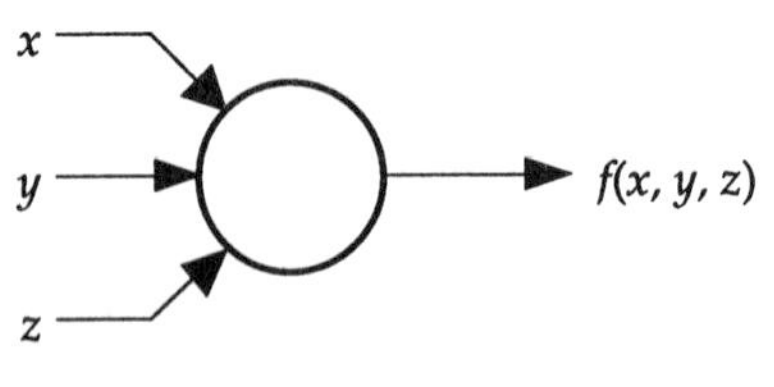


```
REAL32 x, y, z :
SEQ
  PAR
    in.1 ? x
    in.2 ? y
    in.3 ? z
  out ! f(x, y, z)
```

Figure 3.6 Data transformation requires synchronous communication.

Data flow programming is the inverse of control flow (procedural) programming, in which the data flow is implicit. Data flow primitives may, however, be constructed as processes using any programming language that supports synchronous communication. Figure 3.6 shows an example primitive function. This demonstrates that such a language is more *complete* than older languages which fail in this regard.

3.3.3 Data flow programming

We have evolved to communicate using one-dimensional verbal language, but to reason using two-dimensional pictures. Although a procedure is most naturally expressed as a simple list of commands, the dependency of functions upon each other is multi-dimensional. Such data dependencies can, however, be projected onto two dimensions. Data flow may therefore be expressedusing a *visual programming language*.

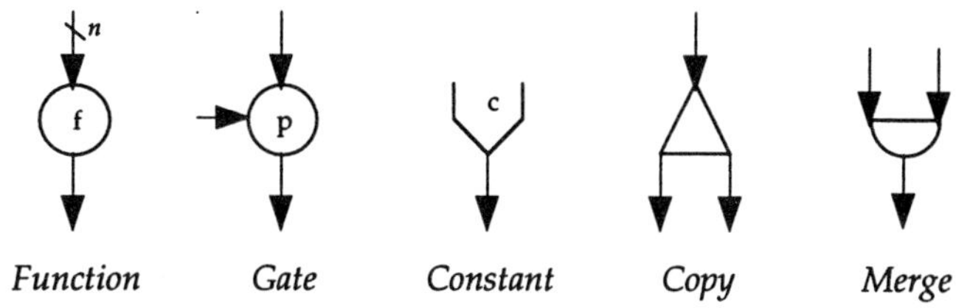

Figure 3.7 Typical primitives of data flow programming.

Figure 3.7 depicts a typical set of primitive operators which either source or transform data. A program is a directed graph where nodes represent operators and edges represent data paths. All communication is synchronous, as is always the case with functional programming. A value of a function cannot be derived until a value for each argument has been received. No function evaluation process may proceed with a subsequent evaluation until the result of the previous evaluation has been successfully communicated. Since all arguments are themselves output from some function evaluation process it follows that all communication must be synchronous. Constant and copy operators are primitive functions (i.e. operators). Merge and gate operators behave in a slightly different manner.

Copy acts as a source. A copy of any datum arriving on its single input emerges on each of its outputs. One new datum has thus been created. Constant also acts as a source, repeatedly generating copies of its statically programmed constant value. A number of function primitives may be expected from the programming environment, as with any programming paradigm. The set offered will depend upon target applications intended by the vendors.

Merge merges two data paths. A datum arriving on either input passes through onto the output. It is then ready to output after just *one* datum received on either input. Gate opens or shuts a connection between its input and output paths according to its programmed predicate, whose truth value depends solely upon its control input. This implies that it may discard a datum input and not be ready to output until its predicate is satisfied and it has subsequently received a datum.

The greater part of the power of functional programming lies in the use of *recursion*. One should expect to find it available in any data flow programming environment. It is left as an exercise for the reader to discover how to employ recursion and the above primitives to implement a function such as *factorial*(x). Note that the function operator, as depicted above, represents not just primitive but also abstract functions.

3.3.4 Object-oriented programming

Over the last few years a new programming paradigm has rapidly gained popularity as a response to the emergence, and increasing social and economic importance, of new applications of computers such as automated manufacture and real-time control of systems, which are often *safety critical*. Software now has to be reusable, more reliable, and therefore modular. Modularity, however, is of two kinds. *Source modularity* refers to the composition of software so that it may be separately developed and validated, and then reused by employing different combinations of modules to create different systems. *Object modularity* refers to the composition of software when it is being executed.

An *object* is a unit of software which has private state and which communicates with other objects via "message passing". It responds to incoming messages by either sending messages of its own or by updating its state. A running object may be regarded as a process and the running program as a directed graph where nodes represent processes and edges represent communication paths. Object modularity may be described thus.

Source modules describe collections of *classes* of object. Each class may *inherit* attributes of another class which offers the possibility of "incremental" programming such that a new class may make use of an existing definition. Existing attributes may even be overridden. Different classes of object may inherit the ability to respond to a particular message from a superclass, but each may respond differently. This property of OOP is called *polymorphism* (literally meaning "many forms"). A commonly quoted example is that of a superclass of graphical objects called `Shape` which responds to the message `draw`. Subclasses `circle` and `square` will respond differently, overriding any response of the parent.

There follows a summary of the properties of OOP.

- Data encapsulation
- Message passing
- Polymorphism
- Inheritance

The big advantage offered by OOP is that it matches the way in which we humans model the world. We create abstractions of everything we encounter which represent only those features which are essential for interaction, or how something changes upon interaction. It is thus both intuitive and infinitely flexible.

It should be pretty obvious how OOP is relevant to parallel programming. It is inherently concurrent. Data encapsulation is just what we need to express domain decomposition. Message passing is exactly what we need to express the synchronous communication between processes. Inheritance just makes it easier and cheaper to create new classes of object.

Despite the fact that OOP was invented in the late 1970s, it has only really gained widespread acceptance in the early 1990s. It demonstrates the hysteresis in the relationship between practical engineering and academic ideas. A new idea has to prove much more than beneficial to be adopted. An old idea has to prove much worse than useless to be dropped.

It is to be hoped that adoption of the OOP paradigm will be accompanied by that of truly appropriate new programming languages[4], not just kludges based upon old ones.

---

1 The term "vector" is inherited from the discipline of mathematics and simply refers to anything which must be specified (e.g. quantified) by *multiple* symbols. For example, a position in space must be specified by *three* numbers and hence is referred to as a vector. By contrast, anything which may be completely specified with a single symbol is referred to as "scalar".

2 The reverse approach, that of attempting to render a highly sequential algorithm more parallel, is extremely difficult and may often be shown to be intractible.

3 The reason is probably that learning a new programming language is perceived as difficult and costly. This is certainly not *necessarily* the case.

4 Ada is an example of an appropriate programing language for OOP which supports all necessary features including concurrency. Version 2 of `occam` lacks explicit source modularity and inheritance. Version 3 is expected shortly to remedy those deficiencies.

Chapter 4

Interconnection Networks

4.1 Static requirements

4.1.1 Symmetry

We need to be able both to express and reason about interconnection networks and their topologies. Luckily, there exists a body of mathematics called Graph Theory which was invented for just such a purpose. Many good books on Graph Theory are available so it is not necessary to review it here. In any case, within the scope of an introductory text such as this one, we do not need to make use of very much theory. However, it is worthwhile to remind ourselves of the basic ideas.

A graph is a set of *nodes* (or *vertices*) which have a *neighbourhood system* which defines the way in which they are connected. Connections between pairs of nodes are called *edges* (or *arcs*). A *directed graph* (or *digraph*) is a graph whose edges possess direction. A *network* is a graph whose edges possess labels or values. Interconnection networks, for our purposes, may be considered to be simple graphs since it is usual to assume that communication between any two connected processor elements is bi-directional. (This is usually necessary to facilitate synchronization.)

A *regular* graph is one in which all nodes share the same *degree* (number of edges). Some, but not all, regular graphs are *vertex symmetric*, meaning that they appear identical from any vertex[1]. Figure 4.1 depicts a regular and vertex symmetric graph. Figure 4.2 depicts a graph which is regular but not vertex symmetric[2].

A *connected* graph is one where a path exists, via a sequence of edges, from every node to every other node. The *connectivity* of any connected graph is the number of edges which must be severed in order to render it *disjoint*, so that one would then have two connected graphs instead of one. Any vertex symmetric regular graph has a connectivity equal to its degree. An interconnection network with high connectivity is desirable for fault-tolerant systems. Such a network is thus desirable since it represents the best connectivity for a given degree and because fault recovery may be an identical process on each node.

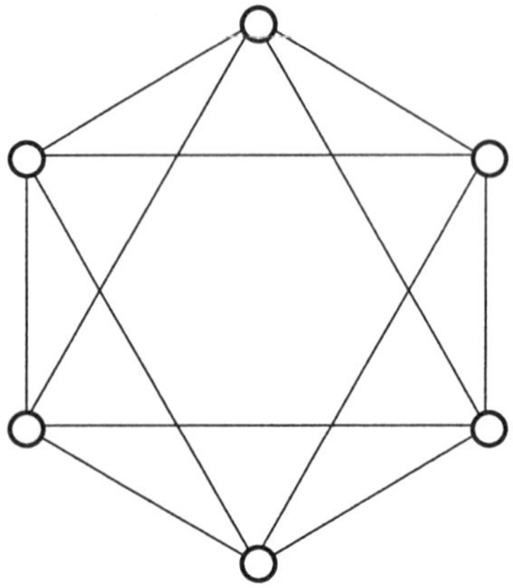

Figure 4.1 A regular and vertex symmetric graph of degree 4.

However, there are reasons why ordinary systems profit from employing a vertex symmetric regular graph too. First, and arguably the most important argument, is that processors (nodes) may be identical. All share a common degree and thus require the same number of communication links. The reason that this is an advantage is that it is cheaper to manufacture many identical items than many different ones. A regular topology alone will not be sufficient to ensure a cheap machine, but it will help to do so.

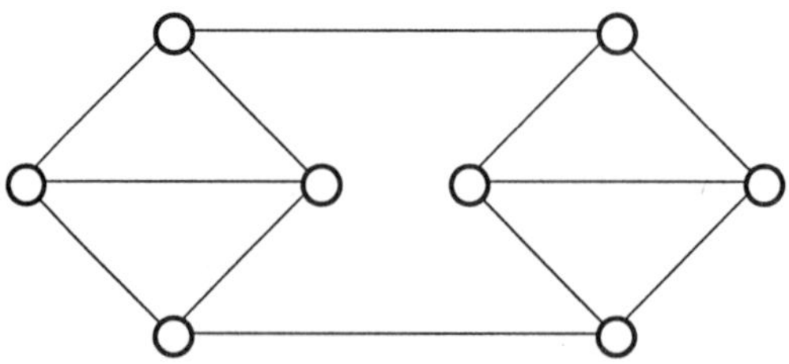

Figure 4.2 A regular graph which is not vertex symmetric.

Secondly, a regular, symmetric topology offers the opportunity to distribute uniformly the communication load. This, in turn, offers the opportunity to reduce traffic congestion to a minimum. A useful analogy for message communication is that of road traffic. Imagine a set of towns connected by roads where each town may accommodate the same size population, and each road is of equal width and quality. In theory, the traffic between any pair of towns depends solely upon the product of the two populations and their distance apart. If we assume that all roads are of equal length then it is only necessary to make them all of one adequate width in order to eliminate traffic congestion completely[3].

Last, a regular, symmetric topology allows the replication of *message-routing* processes. We may define *global communication,* as opposed to purely *local (neighbourhood) communication,* as either of the following.

- Message transfer from one node to any other.
- Message transfer from any node to a server.

If global communication is to be supported then incoming messages may need to be forwarded onto the appropriate output channel. A routing algorithm is required to compute the appropriate output channel, and thus may be the same everywhere *if* the interconnection network is regular.

4.1.2 Flexibility

Any parallel program may be pictured as an *interaction graph* where edges represent communication channels and nodes represent processes, updating purely local state. The process graph must be *embedded* within the interconnection network. Carrying out, or specifying, such an embedding is known as *configuration.*

We therefore require a physical topology for which embeddings are known, or may be derived, for as many process graphs as possible. In practice, an interconnection network is regarded as sufficiently *flexible* if embeddings can be found for the following interaction graphs.

- Ring (pipeline)
- Torus (mesh)
- Binary tree (n'ary tree)

These are perhaps the most common and useful software topologies. The ring and torus are discussed later in this chapter.

Given that an embedding exists, it should be possible to automate it and thus support *declarative* configuration. Ideally, one need only declare the interconnection network and the program and let the development system perform configuration. In practice, it is not quite so easy and such a system is not yet available.

4.1.3 Density and global communication

Here we have yet another requirement which only applies when *global* communication dominates. It does not apply if *local* communication dominates.

The *diameter* of a graph is defined as the maximum distance between any pair of nodes. It may reasonably be assumed that the *average* distance travelled by a message, with either kind of global communication, is approximately proportional to the diameter of the interconnection network. We may refer to the relationship between the diameter and size (number of nodes) of a graph as its *density*. One with low diameter, compared to another of the same size, may be referred to as being more dense.

Clearly, we require a dense topology for an interconnection network in order to minimize communication delays. As we shall analyze a little later, the way in which diameter scales with size will affect the scalability of any network.

4.2 Requirements for scalability

4.2.1 Recursive composition

Scalability is the holy grail of parallel computing. Ideally, when the performance offered by a machine fails to live up to new expectations, it may be scaled to one which succeeds in doing so, without discarding anything.

This requirement clearly requires the interconnection network to be *hierarchically* or *recursively* composed. For example, a pipeline might be defined as being composed of a sequence of pipelines. The recursion may be terminated when we reach the fixed length in which units are manufactured, of perhaps four nodes. It is possible to scale such a machine *linearly*, perhaps expanding by a factor of four with each increment in *order*.

Linear scaling is an example of *geometric* scaling, where the exponent is unity because the network has just one dimension. In other words the network size may be expressed as follows.

$$P \propto n^m \qquad n = order,\quad m = dimension$$

The more general relative of the pipeline is the ring, where the network "wraps around" in one dimension so that it has no end or beginning. It is amusing to consider how this might be perceived by a creature whose entire world is of this topology. Imagine, once again, our friend the ant walking around such a world. It can only stand on one or other node, and can only move to another if there exists an edge between. Such a world is said to be *finite but unbounded*. Our ant never encounters barriers but will soon get bored of seeing the same old nodes, which it can count but cannot tell apart because a ring is vertex symmetric.

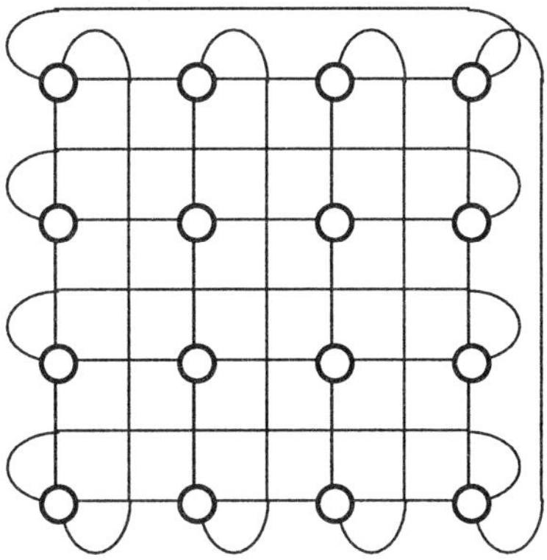

Figure 4.3 Torus as a 2d mesh wrapped around in each dimension.

A torus is very much the same as a ring except it has two dimensions. Just as the pipeline may be wrapped around to form a ring, we may take a 2d mesh and wrap it around in each dimension to form a shape like an American doughnut (or a certain British mint) (Fig.4.3). This time, geometric scaling is to the power of two, and hence network size grows much more rapidly with order. If we consider only tori which are symmetric between dimensions, and define order to equal the number of nodes counted along one dimension, then we have unit constant of proportionality in the equation relating size and order, i.e. $P = n^2$. For example, it tells us that an order 1 network is of size 1, whereas an order 4 network is of size 16.

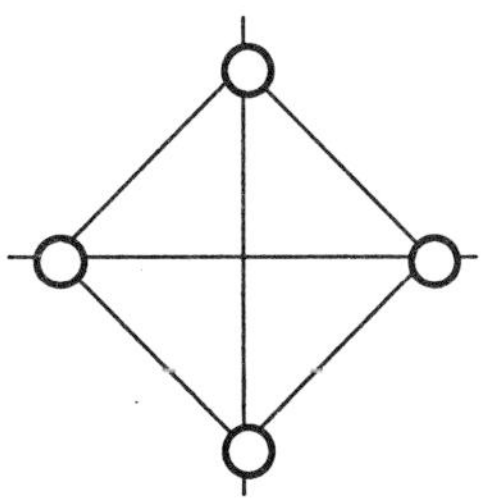

Figure 4.4 Supernode, an example of recursive composition.

The torus cannot be said to possess *recursive* composition, although it can be scaled. Recursive composition means that, on incrementing order, one replaces each node with a sub-network of the same topology. Recursion may be terminated at the outermost level by a wraparound, and at the innermost level by the (atomic) node. Such recursion is only possible if the degree of the fundamental graph, of order 1, is equal to that of the node itself. Figure 4.4 depicts an example known as the "supernode". A supernode of order 1 is shown. To obtain one of order 2 each node is replaced with a copy of the order 1 graph. In general, to obtain the graph of order n one begins with one of order 1 and replaces each node with a graph of order $n - 1$.

Recursive composition leads to *exponential* scaling of size, which may be expressed as follows.

$$P = x^n \qquad x = \textit{size of fundamental (order 1) graph}$$

The important difference between geometric and exponential scaling results from the mathematical fact that an exponential function grows much more quickly than a geometric one. Exponential functions occur in the description of many natural phenomena. (The most well known perhaps is that of unrestrained population growth, as may occur when the normal constraints of predation, limited food supply, and disease are removed[4].) However, there is a function which grows even *more* quickly than an exponential one. There are topologies known which exhibit *factorial* scaling of size with order. One such is known as the *n-star* graph. Table 4.1 below allows comparison of the scaling of size with order for ring, torus, supernode, and n-star. (The reader is encouraged to extrapolate to higher orders.)

Table 4.1 Comparison between geometric, exponential, and factorial scaling of size with order.

		Size		
Order	Ring	Torus	Supernode	N-Star
2	2	4	16	2
3	3	9	64	6
4	4	16	256	24
n	n	n^2	4^n	$n!$

Now we have described all the various possibilities of the scaling of size with order in an interconnection network, we shall turn to think about exactly what we need in this respect. The aims of scaling parallel hardware are two-fold.

- To enable scalable software to be designed so that system efficiency is unaffected, or minimally affected, by scaling hardware.
- To enable the hardware to be scaled without discarding anything and with minimal modification.

Meeting the first aim is the subject of the next section. To meet the second aim we may employ either recursive or extensible topology (such as the torus) for the interconnection network.

There is also the overall aim to meet which is as follows.

- To enable the system (software and hardware) to meet an increase in the performance or domain of the application.

Only here do we find a clue to which class of network size scaling we require. Do application demands scale geometrically, exponentially, or factorially? Suppose we have a machine with 64 processors which becomes insufficient, perhaps due to commercial competition. Is the new performance/cost balance likely to be best satisfied by a new machine with 81 (geometric scaling from 8^2 to 9^2), 256 (exponential scaling from 4^4 to 4^5), or 4096 (factorial scaling) processors?

Factorial scaling is clearly unrealistic. Customers may be willing to pay for three to four times the processing resource, at the low end of scaling, but there will be few applications indeed when they will be willing to pay for 64 times as much in a single step. Geometric scaling is likely to work well – for a while. Exponential scaling is the most effective for most applications providing the mantissa is small. Experience shows that periodic doubling of performance or domain is often required, and is usually at acceptable cost. This is especially evident given that improving technology, and gradual market expansion, reduces the cost of the new equipment anyway.

Exponential scaling, with mantissa 2, of size with order is usually considered ideal.

4.2.2 Communication frequency

Once again we encounter a requirement which constrains the form of the interconnection network only when global communication is dominant.

An assumption which is usually reasonable *but which should be questioned with each application*, as should whether global communication need really dominate design, is as follows.

- Communication demand scales in direct proportion with that for computation.

In other words, we assume that as more computation is performed, the number of messages requiring delivery grows in strict proportion.

(We also assume that average message *size* remains constant.)

If *local* communication dominates demand then the frequency of (fixed length) message transfers increases in direct proportion to the network size.

$$F_c \propto P$$

Local communication
F_c *= communication capacity of entire network*
P = network size

This implies an important consequence.

➤ Local communication implies constant communication demand per processor.

The importance of this conclusion is that, so long as local communication dominates, we may employ the same processor class regardless of scaling. There is an inversion of this which takes account of the fact that there will always be some measure of *global* communication, if only to extract results.

➤ The proportion of communication which is global in nature may determine the acceptable limit to hardware scalability.

Why should global communication cause a problem with scalability of the network? The reason is that, although the quantity of message transfers per process may be constant, *the average distance they travel will increase with network size.* Another assumption is now usually made.

➤ With global communication the average distance traversed by a message scales in proportion with network diameter.

If global communication dominates then the overall frequency of (fixed length) message transfers increases in direct proportion to the *product* of network size and diameter. The bigger the network the more frequently messages must be forwarded.

$$F_c \propto P \times D$$

Global communication
D = network diameter

This leads to the most important conclusion in choosing an interconnection network which offers scalability of global communication.

➤ With global communication, in order to maintain a constant balance between computation and communication when scaling network size, communication capacity per processor must increase in proportion with network diameter.

If we further assume that edges (communication links) in the interconnection network have constant communication capacity, and that the network forms a regular graph, then we may conclude that the communication capacity offered by each processor must scale in direct proportion to the network degree in order to support global communication. Increasing the total communication capacity can thus only be achieved by employing processors with more communication links.

$$f_c \propto d \qquad\qquad \textit{Global communication}$$

$$\Rightarrow \quad d \propto D \qquad\qquad d = \textit{network degree}$$

$$f_c = \textit{communication capacity per processor}$$

Requiring the overall communication capacity per node to scale in proportion with diameter, and recognizing that this will typically imply scaling the network degree in proportion, means that we must seek interconnection networks whose degree equals their diameter as they scale.

➤ With global communication, if the capacity of each communication link cannot be scaled with network size then the topology of the interconnection network must be that of a regular graph of degree directly proportional to diameter, regardless of size.

The implications of these conclusions are far-reaching and profound. It is not possible to understand *any* form of parallel processing without appreciating them. As we concluded in Chapter 1, parallel processing of any kind implies *co-operation*, which in turn implies *communication*, for the purposes of synchronization at least. The above conclusion means, in general terms, that we must seek algorithms in which *local communication dominates!* If we fail to determine such an algorithm then we shall pay a high price for scalability because *each step in scaling will require entirely new hardware*. The requirement of a changed balance between communication and computation capacities will imply a changed design. That in turn implies forfeiting some of the cost benefits of processor mass production. Each distinct network size will require a different class of processor. One cannot simply just add an extra link to every network node upon each scaling step. To do so increases the bus capacity required of the processor which forms the node. That, in turn, affects its entire design. The overall conclusion of this analysis is inescapable.

➤ The dominance of global communication in a parallel algorithm is incompatible with the aim of achieving scalability at low cost.

There is even more bad news for scaling global communication. It has an impact on the demand for computation resource, as well as communication resource. Forwarding a message requires *buffer management* and the execution of the appropriate *routing algorithm*. As the network size increases, message forwarding demands an increasing amount of computation per processor. It becomes more and more important that the routing algorithm be simple and quick to evaluate. Eventually, the overheads of global communication will defeat scalability.

4.3 Specification

4.3.1 occam™ Network Description Language

At present, a typical Network Description Language (NDL) is imperative in nature and reads like a recipe for network construction. The current occam transputer programming environment now incorporates such an NDL. It is instructive to take a brief look at it.

The objects, whose inter-relation is described by NDL code, are as follows.

- Processors, i.e. nodes in an interconnection network. NODE
- Sockets for bi-directional communication links. EDGE
- Bi-directional communication links. ARC

The terms are a little confusing since, in Graph Theory, "edge" and "arc" both mean a connection between two nodes. ("Arc" is sometimes preferred to mean a directed connection and "edge" an undirected one.)

NODEs are declared in a manner similar to that of variables in process specification, and possess attributes which serve to allow the automation, including the compiler, to perform various checks for program and configuration correctness. They include the following.

- Processor type. `[]BYTE type`
- An array of edges. `[]EDGE link`
- Extent of directly addressable memory. `INT memsize`

Each attribute is referenced as an element within a record, e.g. "`pipeNode[2][link][3]`" refers to the link (EDGE) 3 of element 2 in an array of NODEs. With this information, for example, processors of different types (not necessarily all transputers) may be mixed within one network, and an error may be reported if insufficient memory is present on any particular node or if an attempt is made to connect more edges than a particular node possesses.

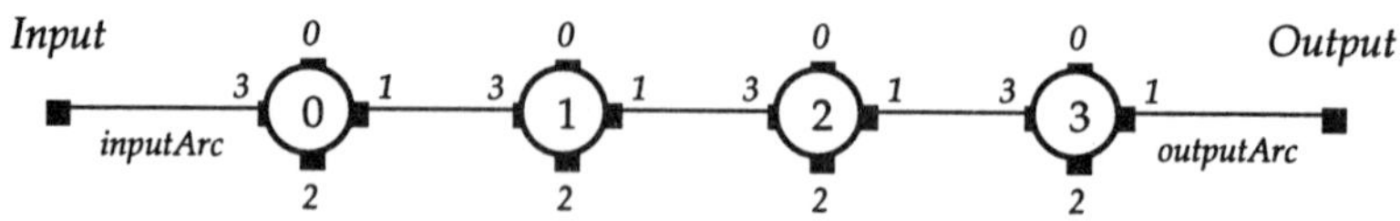

Figure 4.5 A pipeline of processors described by Listing 4.1.

Two primitive operations are provided. SET assigns the attributes of a NODE. The most basic attributes are the type of processor occupying the NODE and the amount of memory it has available. CONNECT assigns an ARC to connect two EDGEs. ARCs assigned between EDGEs of declared NODEs need not be declared and named. EDGEs which represent the boundary of the network, and are thus not an attribute of a declared NODE, *must* be declared. So must the ARCs which connect to them. Listing 4.1 illustrates the NDL program which constructs the pipeline depicted in Figure 4.5.

```
VAL length IS 4 :                  -- Define length
[length]NODE pipeNode :            -- Declare nodes
EDGE input, output :               -- Declare boundaries
ARC inputArc, outputArc :          -- Declare boundary arcs
NETWORK pipeline                   -- Construct pipeline
  DO
    DO i=0 FOR length              -- Set node types
      SET pipeNode[i] (type, memsize := "T805", #100000)
    CONNECT input TO pipeNode[0][link][3] WITH inputArc
    DO i=0 FOR (length-1)          -- Connect them up
      CONNECT pipeNode[i][link][1] TO
              pipeNode[i+1][link][3]
    CONNECT pipeNode[length-1][link][1] TO output
            WITH outputArc
```

Listing 4.1 occam Network Description Language specification of a processor pipeline.

There are two constructors. DO defines a set of construction operations. The order in which statements appear, within a DO scope, is immaterial. (Note that the order in which EDGEs appear in a connect statement is also immaterial.) IF allows the construction of networks which are asymmetric, or which incorporate differing processor (node) types. Its inclusion gives the NDL considerable power of expression.

Expressing a *processor* network, using an NDL, is very much the same kind of programming task as expressing a *process* network, using the configuration language. The reader should thus become a little more confident in expressing hardware topology after reading the later section on configuration.

4.3.2 Cayley Graphs

Declarative specification

Specifying an interconnection network using a Network Description Language, such as described in the last section, leaves a lot to be desired. There is no effective way of reasoning about the network or of discovering its properties. It is quite possible that two different NDL programs may actually describe the same network.

What is actually required is a way of expressing an interconnection network which allows the exploitation of existing mathematical theory. As was stated earlier, Graph Theory is a body of mathematics which represents a lot of useful and relevant knowledge. Because symmetry is of interest, it would also be sensible to find a way of exploiting Group Theory as well. A mathematician called Arthur Cayley related these two bodies of knowledge in a bold and admirable attempt to make learning about groups easier by representing them pictorially, as graphs.

As with Graph Theory, the reader is assumed to have undergone some preparation in Group Theory, but we shall pause for a brief summary of the salient ideas.

Definition of a group

A group may be defined via the combination of two ideas.

- A set of elements.
- A binary operation on the set.

The combination of set and operator must satisfy three group axioms in order to qualify as a group. "$\bullet$" denotes the binary operator. Letters represent members of the set. The combination of two members via the operator is usually referred to as their "product" or "composition".

- Associativity $a \bullet (b \bullet c) = (a \bullet b) \bullet c$
- Identity $a \bullet I = I \bullet a = a$
- Inverse $a \bullet a^{-1} = a^{-1} \bullet a = I$

The reason why most of us consider mathematics difficult is most probably because it is about pure abstraction. Those who display an aptitude for the subject do so by showing that they are happy with pure abstraction, with little need to relate ideas to specific objects and events. Such people are mathematicians by nature. The rest of us should look for illustrations of mathematical ideas to find satisfaction.

The idea of a group is typical. Members of a group set may represent numbers, propositions, pieces of fruit – *anything,* as long as the group operator produces another member of the set. Consider a set of puddings together with a "mix two together" operator. For example, ice-cream and mango may both be members of the set of puddings, *as are their mixture.*

An operator is said to be *associative* if the order in which evaluation occurs makes no difference to the outcome. Suppose we mix ice-cream first with mango and then mix the result with chocolate sauce. We get the same pudding if we mix the mango and chocolate sauce first instead and only then combine the result with ice-cream.

For the combination of set and operator to qualify as a group, we must be able to find a unique member (I) which satisfies the *identity* axiom. Here we have a problem with puddings. It is doubtful that a pudding can be found that, when mixed with any other, leaves it unchanged. A more useful example is simple arithmetic, where the set is that of positive integers, and the operator is addition. It is easy to show that addition of positive integers is associative. It is also easy to show that zero satisfies the identity axiom. Add zero to any positive integer, or vice versa, and it is left unchanged.

The set of positive integers under addition is *not* a group because no inverse exists for any member except zero. To satisfy all three group axioms we must look to the set of *all* integers under addition. The inverse of any member is just its negative. To find the inverse of any integer, we just look for a partner such that the operator yields zero, regardless of order. It would not be so easy to determine the appropriate set to form a group under multiplication. There, to satisfy the third axiom, we would need the set to include all rational fractions. In fact, numbers may be loosely defined as the union of those sets which satisfy the group axioms for a given set of numerical operators[5].

Group generators and relations

It is sometimes difficult or awkward to express a group as the combination of set and operator, especially if one wishes to be exact. For example, the set concerned may be very large, or even infinite. There is an alternative.

If we start with any element, sometimes we can get the same product in different ways. Some compositions take us back where we began and are thus said to form a cycle. We can express such possibilities by using the same notation as is used in algebra to express a power.

$$a \bullet a = a^2$$

$$a \bullet a \bullet a = a^3$$

etc.

For example, we may express that composing any member of the group with element b five times yields the same element as doing so with element a three times as follows.

$$a^3 = b^5$$

Cycles of length n in the group may be expressed as the equivalence between composing with given elements a total of n times and doing so once with the identity element. Such an equivalence is known as a *group relation*.

$$a^p b^q = I \mid p + q = n$$

It is often possible to find a small set of elements within the group from which all others may be generated by composition. If so, the subset

$\{g_i\}$ of elements are known as *generators* of the group. A minimum set of relations between the generators via which every group member may be generated is known as the *defining relations*. An example of the specification of a family of groups in this way is as follows.

$$G_n = \left\langle \{a,b\} \middle| a^n = b^2, a^{2n} = I, bab = a^{-1} \right\rangle$$

Cayley Graph of a group

We think best in pictures. When learning, pictures are worth much more than a thousand words. This is why Arthur Cayley decided to exploit the similarity in the definitions of group and graph in his teaching.

The *Cayley Graph* of a given group has nodes which correspond to group members and edges which correspond to the *action* of each generator. Starting from any node, it is possible to traverse the entire graph, and thus visit every node, by following the action of the generators. It is thus implicit that the graph is both regular and vertex symmetric. In fact, Cayley Graphs sport just about every property which we require for an interconnection network.

- Every Cayley Graph is regular and vertex symmetric.
- The degree of a Cayley Graph equals the number of generators and their inverses.
- The length of a cycle equals the order of the associated identity relation.
- The shortest path, and thus the routing algorithm, may be deduced by formal methods.

We may additionally choose defining relations which express any symmetry we may desire. It seems almost too good to be true, but such gems lurk everywhere in the annals of mathematics.

4.3.3 Hypercube as Cayley Graph

We now seize the opportunity to describe an interconnection network topology which is arguably the most successful to date: the hypercube.

It was decided earlier that an ideal size scaling was exponential with base 2. The simplest set of elements to choose would then be n copies of a set of two symbols. We add just one other requirement, that of binary symmetry. If a message arrives on a given edge then an acknowledgement may be returned over that same edge. In group terms, this may be expressed as requiring a cycle of length 2 for each generator. The group may be expressed as follows.

$$G_n = \left\langle \{g_i\}, 1 \le i \le n \middle| {g_i}^2 = I = (g_i g_j)^2 \right\rangle \qquad n = order$$

Choosing to employ n copies of the symbols {0,1} by which to label the group members, and thus the nodes in our graph, is equivalent to employing an n-bit binary number. A suitable instance of the desired group is then just the set of n-bit binary numbers under the exclusive OR ($\oplus$) operator. The generators thus correspond to the subset of elements with just one digit equal to 1. It is possible to generate the rest of the group by combining generators via the $\oplus$ operator. For example, with order $n = 3$ the generators are {001, 010, 100} and the remaining member elements may be generated as follows.

$$
\begin{aligned}
001 \oplus 001 &= 000 \\
001 \oplus 010 &= 011 \\
001 \oplus 100 &= 101 \\
010 \oplus 100 &= 110 \\
001 \oplus 010 \oplus 100 &= 111
\end{aligned}
$$

To see what this graph looks like, we begin with any node and draw the action of the generators. Figure 4.6 shows the hypercube graph for orders 1 and 2. Figure 4.7 shows order 3 and 4 hypercubes, and how the hypercube earns its name.

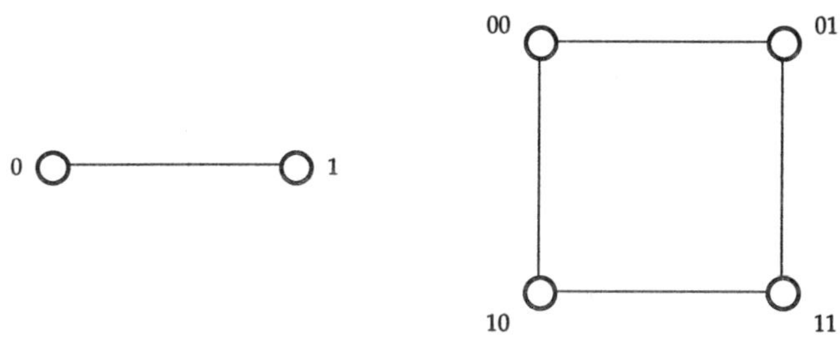

Figure 4.6 Hypercubes of orders 1 and 2.

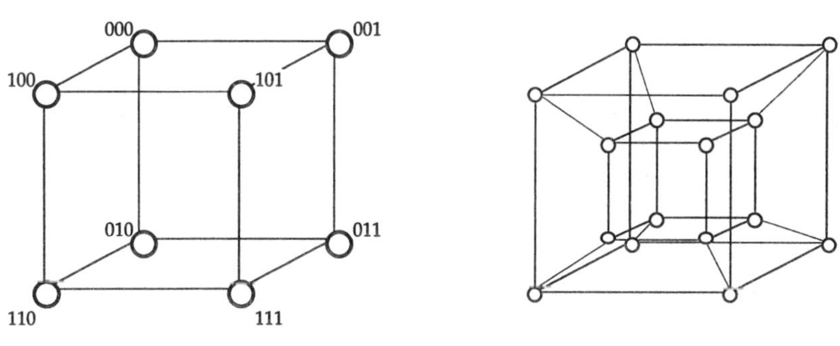

Figure 4.7 Hypercubes of orders 3 and 4.

Each increment in order requires an extra digit for each label. It should be clear from the figure that hypercubes possess *hierarchical* composition. One is constructed by connecting the corresponding nodes of two copies of one of the previous order. Degree and diameter equal order. Hypercube properties may be summarized as follows.

$$P = 2^n$$

$$D = n = \log_2 P \qquad n = order$$

$$d = n = \log_2 P$$

Scaling of both population (size) and diameter is ideal. The equality of diameter and degree also ideally supports use of a standard communication link, as decided earlier. The only setback is that a common, standard processor cannot be economically employed for networks of different order. (See Section 4.2.)

Each link is associated with a generator. Anywhere in the network, one can tell the identity of the node on the other side of a link by the action of the corresponding generator. For example, the generator corresponding to link 0 has only bit 0 set. Thus the identity of the node on the other side of "dimension 0" is the same as the local one except for having bit 0 "flipped".

Messages are assumed to incorporate a header which in turn includes destination node identity. The distance a message must travel equals the number of bits which differ between source and destination node identities (known as the *Hamming distance*) since each differing bit must be flipped, requiring the action of one generator.

4.4 Configuration

4.4.1 Automated versus programmed configuration

Programming means specifying the behaviour of a machine. One difference between programming a parallel machine and programming a purely sequential one is that the machine topology (and even its architecture) can vary. Ideally, it should only be necessary to specify the desired behaviour and employ automation to exploit prior knowledge of the machine to bring about such behaviour. Such portability of software is not yet a commercial reality for *sequential* machines, even though it is technically straightforward. Portability between different *parallel* architectures is still a matter for research and will rely on determining the most effective common model for parallel computation (and getting everyone to agree on it). Portability between parallel machines of common architecture but merely different interconnection networks *is* often possible.

A parallel programming environment must support the following three phases of system behaviour specification.

- Processors and their interconnection: *network description*
- Mapping of software onto hardware: *configuration*
- Behaviour of processes and their interconnection: *programming*

Configuration could, in theory, be automated, even to the extent of optimization. Graph Theory might be employed to seek an *embedding* of the process interaction graph into the processor interconnection network. Configuration is usually equivalent to the merging of processes until each node represents the complete behaviour of a processor. The code which requires loading onto each processor is then rendered explicit.

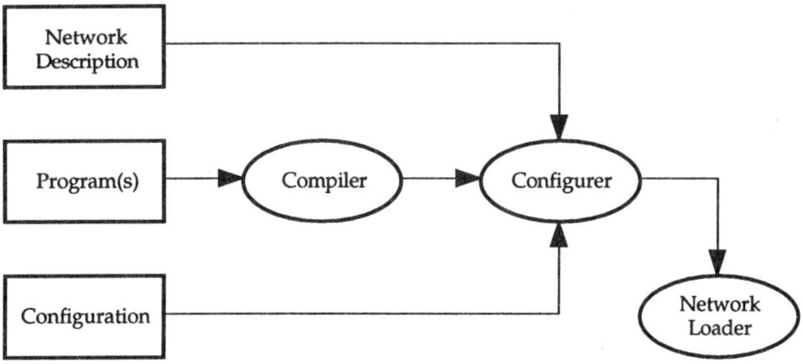

Figure 4.8 Data flow diagram for the life-cycle of a parallel program.

The purpose of configuration is to assert a mapping between software and hardware. Processes must be assigned to processors and channels must be assigned to links. It may be necessary to dictate that certain processes be assigned to specific processors, perhaps because they are bound to special hardware. Another, more common, reason why configuration is not automated is simply that such automation may not exist or may not offer optimum performance.

The development system depicted in Figure 4.8 assumes that the compiler sends compiled processes to the configurer, which then requires a configuration to define which process is placed upon each processor described in the network description. Even if the configuration is to be automatic, the configurer still requires a description of process interconnection, rather than the executable code which a compiler is designed to produce, in order to map software onto hardware.

4.4.2 Configuration and code loading

Whether derived by human or by automation, configuration must uniquely specify the action of a *Network Loader*, whose job it is to initialize the state of (bootstrap) each processor, and then load and enter the machine code for the process which is to run on it. It is well worth a brief review of the operation of a Network Loader.

A Network Loader is simply a program which is entered by a *root* processor which has access to a file server. It reads a file which is an *image* of the entire configured network program. The image consists of a list of operations (Network Loader commands) and operands, much like an "executable" image for a purely sequential system with just one processor. Operands are typically just blocks of data. Operations include the following.

- Bootstrap processor connected to <link>.
- Transmit Network Loader down <link>.
- Transmit <data> down <link>.
- Load <data> into memory.
- Terminate Network Loader.

A copy of the Network Loader is loaded and run on each processor. Processor initialization and code loading can be arranged such that the correct process is entered upon its termination. Data subsequently transmitted down a link to a neighbouring processor contain Network Loader commands, thus facilitating code loading and entry across the entire network.

4.4.3 Programmed configuration

Domain decomposition will often imply process replication. It is then possible to proceed by first programming the process to be replicated, one copy per processor, and specifying the interconnection of the multiple instances within the configuration. Such a configuration implies two constraints.

- A semi-Hamiltonian path (i.e. a path which visits each node just once) must be found.
- A consistent edge labelling scheme must be devised.

The required configuration may then be derived via the following procedure, assuming that the process/processor network represents a known Cayley Graph, and that a two-dimensional array of channels is declared to connect the processes. The size required in each dimension is equal to the size and degree of the network respectively.

1 Employ a replicated `PAR` whose index enumerates processors along the semi-Hamiltonian path.
2 Label output channels according to replication index and generator.

3 Label input channels according to the generator and the product of replication index and generator.

It should be noted that processes may be replicated and interconnected in a semantically identical way within a single program, allowing the compiler to produce a single compiled process, thus executable only on a *single* processor. The job of the configurer is to permit the execution of a program upon *multiple* processors by creating an appropriate sequence of commands and data for the Network Loader.

4.4.4 Example programmed configurations

Ring

A ring processor topology is common and has the following properties.

- Fixed degree = 2.
- Linear (geometric) scaling of size P.
- Diameter = P/2.
- Low connectivity = 2.
- Simple, efficient routing algorithm.

We assume replication of a process, of degree 2, named `worker`. A semi-Hamiltonian path obviously exists, so we proceed to name outgoing channels according to replication index and link. (The Cayley Graph is not needed in such a simple example.) Listing 4.2 shows the configuration using occam configuration language.

```
VAL P IS 8 :                              -- Define size
CONFIG
  [P][2]CHAN OF MyProtocol edge :         -- Declare channels
  PAR i=0 FOR P                           -- Replicate
    PROCESSOR Ring[i]
      worker(edge[((i+P)-1) REM P,1],     -- Reverse input
             edge[i,0],                   -- Reverse output
             edge[(i+1) REM P, 0],        -- Forward input
             edge[i,1])                   -- Forward output
```

Listing 4.2 Programmed configuration of process ring onto processor ring.

It is assumed that the configurer is sufficiently "intelligent" that it can map channels onto processor links without any human help. The processor identifier `Ring` is assumed defined in an appropriate network description. The edge (channel) labelling is consistent and allows actual channel parameter indices to be computed at configuration time (via modulo arithmetic).

Torus

Torus topology is also popular since it offers a match to commonly encountered two-dimensional domain decomposition. Having degree 4, it provides an obvious match to processors with four links, such as the Inmos Transputer.

- Fixed degree = 4.
- Geometric scaling of size P = X × Y.
- Diameter = (X DIV 2) + (Y DIV 2).
- Connectivity = 4.
- Simple, efficient routing algorithm.

A semi-Hamiltonian path exists which corresponds exactly to the unfolding of a two-dimensional array into one dimension. (Imagine iteratively following the first index around the first dimension and then incrementing the second index.) Hence we may employ two nested replicated PAR constructors. Again, we compose the channels ordered by link and direction (Listing 4.3).

```
VAL X IS 4 :        -- Define size of network
VAL Y IS 8 :        -- in each dimension
CONFIG
  [X][Y][4]CHAN OF MyProtocol edge :  -- Declare channels
  PAR i=0 FOR X    -- Replicate along X axis
    PAR j=0 FOR Y -- Replicate along Y axis
      PROCESSOR Torus[i,j]
        worker(edge[i, ((j+Y)-1) REM Y, 2], edge[i, j, 0],
               edge[(i+1) REM X, j, 3], edge[i, j, 1],
               edge[i, (j+1) REM Y, 0], edge[i, j, 2],
               edge[((i+X)-1) REM X, j, 1], edge[i, j, 3])
```

Listing 4.3 Programmed configuration of a torus.

Once again there exists no need for Cayley Graph representation. It is easy to work out intuitively the expression which computes (at configuration time) the identity of the processor on the other end of each input channel, and thus that of the channel itself. Note that, as with the ring configuration above, this configuration is scalable.

Hypercube

The hypercube represents a more interesting example as it illustrates how configuration is made easier by reference to the Cayley Graph metaphor.

- Degree = order = N.
- Exponential scaling of size P = 2^N.
- Diameter = N.

- Connectivity = N.
- Simple, efficient routing algorithm.

This time it is *not* possible to compose configuration in a scalable way because the degree varies with order. It *is* possible to compose the worker process in a manner applicable to any order provided the implementation language permits variable size array parameters and the recovery of array size at run-time, as is the case with occam. The editing required to correct the configuration for order is minor. (An edit is required anyway to adjust the order definition.) An array of input channels must be constructed as appropriate to the order. The appropriate array of output channels may be simply selected by the first array index (Listing 4.4).

```
VAL N IS 4 :                          -- Define order
VAL P IS 1 << N :                     -- Compute size
CONFIG
  [P][N]CHAN OF MyProtocol edge :     -- Declare channels
  PAR i=0 FOR P                       -- Replicate
    PROCESSOR Hypercube[i]
      worker([edge[i >< 1, 0], edge[i >< 2, 1],
              edge[i >< 4, 2], edge[i >< 8, 3]],
             edge[i])
```

Listing 4.4 Programmed configuration of hypercube.

It is possible to show that a semi-Hamiltonian path does indeed exist in a hypercube graph. As long as we know it exists we know that code loading is possible and may simply make use of the enumeration along that path in order to reference each processor and thus each channel. To determine the identity of channels connected to the inputs of each node we make use of the fact that a hypercube represents a Cayley Graph as described in Section 4.3.3.

It is easy to make use of the instance of the underlying group whose membership is made up of n copies of {0, 1}, i.e. all possible values of an n-bit binary number, and the exclusive OR operator (represented in occam by "><"). The generators of such a group are just those n-bit binary numbers that possess just one digit equal to 1. Readers are strongly recommended to satisfy themselves that all members of the group may be generated as products of the generators alone.

Nodes correspond to members of the group. Their interconnection corresponds to the action of generators. The symmetry that characterizes the hypercube may now be perceived. Any generator squared equals the identity element, which is represented here by a string of n zeros. If we leave any node along a chosen channel and then leave the destination node along a channel of the same index we shall arrive back where we started from. It is equivalent to composing any group element with any one generator twice and thus to composing that same element with the identity element. It will be left unchanged. In other words, we end up where we started from.

It is this binary symmetry that allows the determination of the identity of channels input to any node. All generators are the same as their inverses. All that is necessary to compute the identity of the source node, and thus the channel identity, is to compose the node label with the generator corresponding to that input port.

Final word

These examples illustrate how configuration is used to describe the interconnection of processes in such a way that a description of code loading (configuration "image") may be derived. It is also usually not the case that practical systems can be built with replication alone. Real systems typically require modification to include configuration of at least one special process which provides services (e.g. file or terminal services). In other words, in real life things usually get a lot more messy!

---

1 Imagine you are an ant walking around the graph. If the graph is vertex symmetric then you will have no way of knowing where you are. Whichever vertex you are standing on, the graph appears the same.

2 My thanks to my colleague Dr Sabah Jassim for the suggested illustration.

3 Unfortunately for those whose responsibility it is to plan transport infrastructure, things are never quite so simple.

4 Experiments with rats indicates that, when the natural constraints of limited resources and predation are removed, social (co-operative) behaviour becomes less common and anti-social behaviour becomes more common. Anti-social behaviour may even sink to the level of cannibalism. The result is a declining population. It is not known whether nature has ever had to resort to this response to restrain or reverse population growth. Disease is usually effective. Let us all hope that, as a species, we choose voluntary restraint!

5 The reader is warned that the water gets a bit deeper before a complete and satisfying definition may be found. The allusion here is purely illustrative.

Chapter 5

Communication and Scalability

5.1 Communication infrastructure

5.1.1 Object-oriented design

The purpose of this entire book is not to review all possible methods of processing information in parallel, but to focus on fundamental and unavoidable issues and try to impart some real technical capability to the reader. So we now turn to the engineering of software for parallel processing systems which possess distributed memory and employ Communicating Process Architecture.

Engineering software differs from engineering mechanical systems in that applications cannot be easily categorized. For example, in mechanical engineering special study can be devoted to the design of bridges. An engineer responsible for the design of a new bridge can take advantage of great expertise in bridge design, built up over many generations. The best that can be done to assist software design is to accumulate *classes* of software *objects* which may be refined for use across a range of applications. Object-oriented software design has now largely replaced earlier techniques and promises some similar measure of reliability to that taken for granted in mechanical or electronic systems.

It is beyond the scope of this text to discuss the principles of object-oriented design but a brief summary is useful. The salient principles are as follows.

- Communication ("message passing")
- Encapsulation
- Polymorphism
- Inheritance

Object-oriented software source code describes classes of objects which mimic the behaviour of *abstractions*[1] of objects in the real world. Classes are usually defined in terms of others which possess a greater degree of abstraction. They *inherit* features from their ancestors. Each object is capable of communicating according to a specified protocol and may be defined solely according to its behaviour upon receipt of a message, whereupon it may update its internal state and/or send messages to other objects. All information is *encapsulated,* and only locally accessible. No information is globally accessible. Two objects may share the inherited ability to respond to a particular message but each may respond to it in different ways. Behaviour is thus said to be *polymorphic* (able to take many forms).

All objects may be defined so as to be entirely passive. They then speak not until spoken to. This may seem strange to anyone taught programming in what is unfortunately the traditional pattern, i.e. a list of commands which are obeyed by the machine in the order given, no matter what. In fact, *event driven* systems are often much more natural. A WIMP[2] human/computer interface to a program forces it to be event driven and thus much easier for the user to operate. It is, for example, most natural and intuitive for a word processor to do nothing until the user presses the mouse button or a character key. The user is in control and not the machine, as should be the case.

We shall see, in the next chapter, that passiveness can be a powerful design rule since it can guarantee freedom from deadlock. However, it is not a necessity. In fact, it severely constrains the way in which systems are designed. Most so-called object-oriented programming languages make it impossible to implement *active* objects, which possess their own thread of control[3]. occam has no such limitation.

Object-oriented software design is better suited to parallel software than it is to the (traditional) purely sequential kind. A process is simply a running object. Expressing desired system behaviour as a network of communicating objects thus assumes the existence of multiple real or *virtual* processors. However, one pertinent comment must be made about programming languages referred to as object-oriented. Communication in most such languages is achieved using the mechanism of procedure invocation. This is synchronous, as required for generality[4], but renders program structure obscure compared to that easily achieved with a language which incorporates synchronous communication as primitive. occam currently lacks the ability to express inheritance but does incorporate primitives for the explicit expression of synchronous communication. It also offers encapsulation and polymorphism in a simple and natural way. It is thus an ideal language in which to express parallel algorithms, though not source modularity, within an object-oriented framework.

5.1.2 Virtual communication

Earlier in this book it was pointed out that software decomposition could be achieved either by function or by domain, and that process allocation could be achieved either statically or dynamically (by farming) (Fig. 5.1). Deciding between these options is the first step in designing a parallel software system.

		Scheduling	
		Static	*Dynamic*
Decomposition	*Function*		
	Domain		

Figure 5.1 The parallel decomposition matrix.

Once that decision has been made the next step is to design and construct a *virtual communication architecture* for the system. The purpose of such a step is to separate the concerns of data transformation and communication. Once constructed (and validated[5]) such a system may often be re-used in future applications, thus achieving a primary aim of software modularity. It is the purpose of this chapter and the next to discuss the requirements of, and problems inherent in, a virtual communication architecture.

It may be helpful now to review the kinds of communication which may be required. *Local* communication is simply that between neighbours. *Global* communication is that between processes which are not necessarily neighbours, and may usefully be subdivided into two classes. The first is where one party is special in that it provides a *service* of some kind. The second covers all other communication, where either party may lie anywhere within the network.

A virtual communication architecture that is limited to purely local communication permits each node to interact (exchange messages) only with its neighbours. One that supports global node-to-server communication allows each node to interact with at least one server. Finally, one that supports the luxury of full global node-to-node communication allows each node to interact with *any* other it may choose.

We will now discuss some implications of the decomposition and allocation decisions for the virtual communication architecture.

5.1.3 Communication architecture

Farm

Farming was introduced in Chapter 1 and represents any system where the allocation of processes to processors is done dynamically, i.e. at run-time. In its simplest form a "farmer" allocates tasks to replicated "workers".

From the point of view of communication, a farmer represents a server providing shared access to a pool of work. We thus require implementation of global node-to-server communication. For efficiency's sake, on starting, the farmer may assume a request for work from each and every worker, and must therefore know how many of them there are. Subsequently, a fresh work packet is issued following the arrival of each packet of results. There exists no requirement for general node-to-node communication, there being no inherent need for workers to communicate with each other, except to forward work when busy.

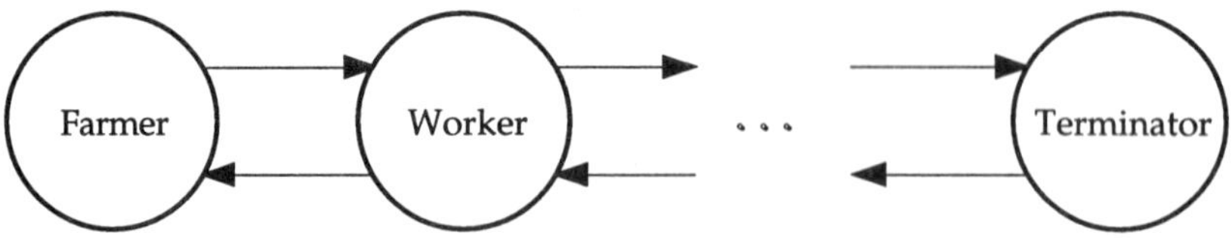

Figure 5.2 Farming a pipeline of processors.

The direct connection of every worker renders the farmer somewhat difficult to implement, particularly with regard to hardware where the number of physical channels per processor is limited. Farming is usually implemented on a hierarchical interconnection network. The simplest example is that of a pipeline as depicted in Figure 5.2. Here, we have a farmer and a number of replicated worker processes embedded within a suitable communication architecture which supports the distribution of work packets. Figure 5.3 depicts the embedding of the worker process within its associated communication support process.

There are certain processes which prove ubiquitous when implementing communication architectures. A *multiplexor* (MUX) possesses multiple input channels but only one output channel. Any message arriving at any input channel will appear on the output channel. Messages should appear on the output channel in the same order as they arrive. A *demultiplexor* (DEMUX) performs the inverse job and has multiple output channels but only one input channel. Messages arriving on the input channel appear on an output channel decided according to some specified protocol. In some demultiplexors message content will decide the selection of output. Alternatively, outputs may be ordered according to priority and a newly arrived message will be output onto the highest-priority channel which is ready to communicate.

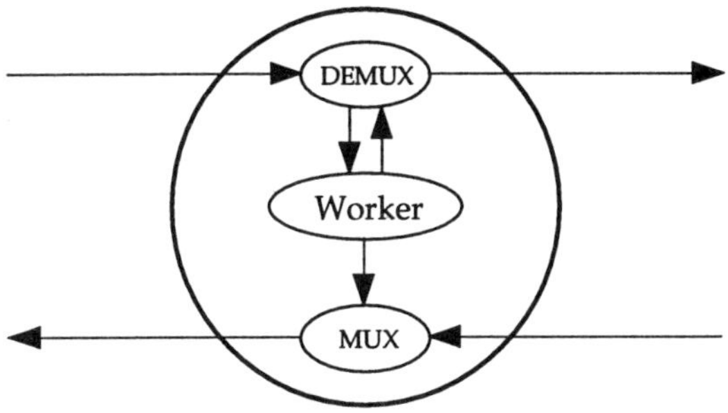

Figure 5.3 Replicated work node process in a processor pipeline.

In practice, the implementation of output guards is computationally expensive. This is why occam only offers selection by ready input in its guarded selection construct (ALT). The problem must be overcome at the design phase by adding extra channels to make the demultiplexor *demand driven* as shown on the right in Listing 5.1. An incoming message is now output on the highest-priority channel for which a request for data has been made.

```
WHILE TRUE                          WHILE TRUE
  SEQ                                 SEQ
    in ? message                        in ? message
    PRI ALT i=0 FOR N                   PRI ALT i=0 FOR N
      out[i] ! message                    out.request[i] ? any
        SKIP                                out[i] ! message
```

Listing 5.1 Demultiplexor (DEMUX) process with output and input guards respectively.

The demultiplexor in Figure 5.3 is a slight variation. It employs an output request channel only for its high-priority output. If, after receiving a message, no output request for the high-priority channel is found awaiting a response then the packet is output on the low-priority channel. The worker is presumed already busy. Listing 5.2 shows how this may be achieved.

For an incoming work packet, giving highest priority to the local worker means that work is allocated to those workers nearest the farmer first. This reduces the overhead of distributing work.

The multiplexor merely collects results from the worker, and from workers further down the pipeline, and forwards them up the pipeline. The pipeline must have an appropriate process added at its end in order to satisfy the communication expectations of the final worker. Note that each demultiplexor may act as a buffer for one work packet.

```
WHILE TRUE
  SEQ
    in ? work
    PRI ALT
      out.request ? any        -- Request for hi pri o/p?
        out[0] ! work
      SKIP                     -- Lo pri o/p always ready
        out[1] ! work
```

Listing 5.2 Modified demultiplexor process depicted in Figure 5.3.

The farmer has the job of decomposing the computation to be performed into work packets. As a result, its structure will depend heavily upon the application. However, as far as the communication architecture is concerned, the structure must give priority to keeping all workers busy as much of the time as possible.

The design relies on work packets *not* being dispensed by the farmer unless at least one worker is free. Otherwise it would be possible for the demultiplexors to *block* each other, thus possibly preventing a newly free worker receiving fresh work. Deadlock might eventually occur.

Security may be guaranteed if a proper *client/server* protocol[6] is maintained. Initially, one packet of work is despatched for each worker. Additional work must then be sent only after the server has received a request, in the form of a "results" packet. The farmer must guarantee always to accept a request for more work, and each worker must guarantee to accept the work it has requested.

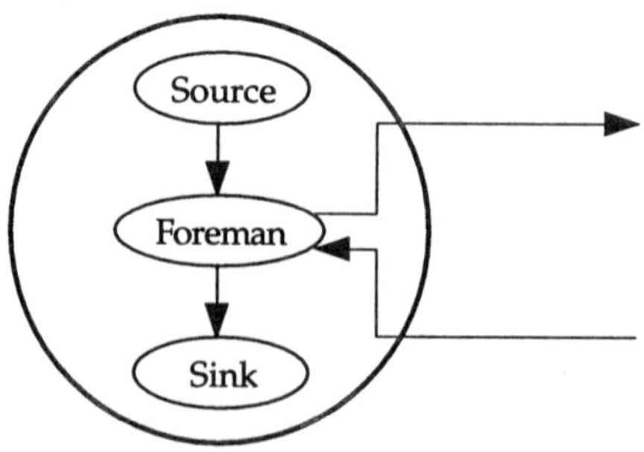

Figure 5.4 Decomposition of farmer process.

Implementing a client/server protocol is straightforward if the source of work and the sink for results are independent of one another. Figure 5.4 shows such a structure and Listing 5.3 shows how the "Foreman" process might guarantee secure service assuming that `free.workers` is initialized to the workforce size.

```
WHILE TRUE
  PRI ALT
    free.workers > 0 & from.source ? work
      SEQ                        -- Refuse new work if all
        to.workers ! work        -- workers busy
        free.workers := free.workers - 1
    from.workers ? results
      SEQ                        -- Collect results and
        to.sink ! results        -- pass on to sink
        free.workers := free.workers + 1
```

Listing 5.3 Foreman process regulates workload by acting as a server of work packets.

Life becomes a little more complicated if new work depends upon the results of old (implying an extra channel between sink and source). Satisfying a request for more work might imply awaiting the arrival of more results. However, because the foreman continues to accept requests, even though it has some outstanding, it is possible to prove that each one will eventually be satisfied[7].

Cellular array

For a second example of virtual communication architecture design we shall now consider an array of cyclic processes whose communication is predominantly both synchronous and local. Such an array may have any number of dimensions but it may help if we consider one of just two dimensions because it is easiest to visualize. If bounded such a system would be called a grid and will not afford the luxury of straightforward replication. (Boundary processes have special behaviour, hence so do their neighbours, and so on.) A two-dimensional array, which is finite but unbounded, is called a *torus*[8].

An array of cyclic processes computing via purely local synchronous interaction may be referred to as *systolic*[9] when information flows across the surface from source to sink like blood around a body. Because of the lack of global communication the systolic array makes a very effective model for *scalable* parallel software systems. There are two other possibilities for information flow.

- Third dimension: each and every process has the capability of receiving and/or sending data along a third (extra) dimension.
- Node-to-server global communication: each and every process supports a message-router.

If information is to flow in and out of the system then there has to exist access to channels connected to and from the external environment. In the first possibility listed above, every process is connected to at least one such channel. The simplest example is where the information to be processed is distributed statically, prior to system start ("off-line"), so that no input channels are required. Each process has one output channel, in the third dimension, along which it may send results. The simplest output channel might just be a single pixel on a visual display. Each output value may depend upon the state of the process and that of its neighbours.

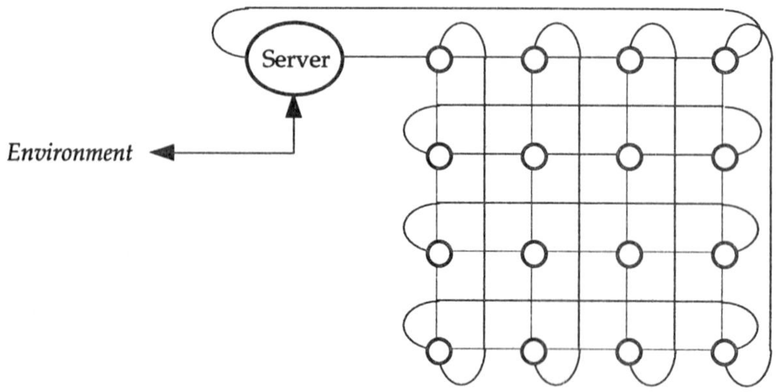

Figure 5.5 A process torus with added server node.

The second possibility requires the presence of server processes within the network which provide access to environment channels. The simplest case is for there to exist just one unified server providing access to both input and output channels. Replication of processes or processors is made simpler if the server location is hidden, e.g. Figure 5.5. All nodes within the torus may thus be identical and only the server special. Messages which form part of the local interaction are transferred directly across the server rendering it transparent to the computing surface. It acts only as a source or sink for messages which form global node-to-server interaction.

The advantage of this method is that it does not require a channel directly connected between each process and an output sink. It is thus much easier to scale, particularly with regard to hardware. However, it is at the cost of increased complexity of the process to be replicated. Although global communication has been introduced, the frequency with which it is used may usually be kept small compared to that of local communication. Scalability is not then unduly impaired. If possible, the amount of service requested should be kept constant as the network scales in size. Figure 5.6 depicts the required architecture of the replicated process in order to support global communication with the unified server. To keep the diagram simple it shows internal channels connecting just one demultiplexor to output multiplexors and the local worker. Demultiplexors and multiplexors may be internally replicated. The routing algorithm must be incorporated within the demultiplexor.

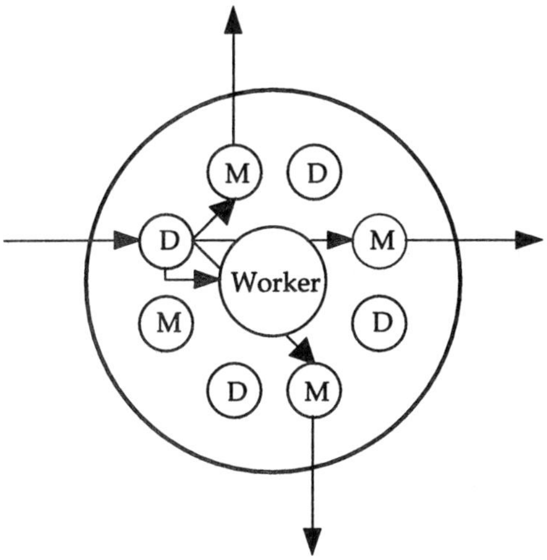

Figure 5.6 Process communication architecture to support message routing.

5.1.4 Termination and reset

Insecure termination

It has so far been universally assumed that all processes run without ever terminating. This has made it easy to describe the behaviour of simple component processes within a virtual communication architecture. If, on the other hand, a system specification requires the ability to terminate then great care must be given to ensure valid design. First let us state the problem clearly and without ambiguity.

Q How do we arrange secure termination of an entire arbitrary process network, initiated either by a component process or by the environment?

Termination may be of some or all processes within a system. It may be initiated by a signal from the system environment or by a process within the network.

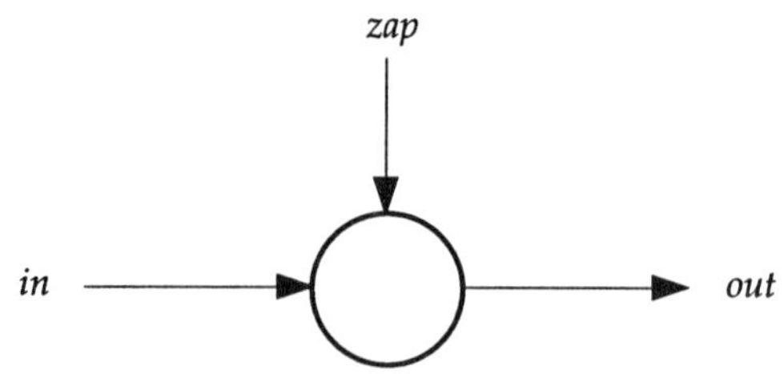

Figure 5.7 Simple data transform process with termination channel.

So why is this such a big problem? To see why, consider the simple but typical example shown in Figure 5.7. A process iteratively accepts data on a single input channel, processes it, and then outputs the result.

```
WHILE running
  ALT
    in ? data
      SEQ                         -- If data arrived then
        ... compute result        -- process them and
        out ! result              -- output result
    zap ? any                     -- If termination signal
      running := FALSE            -- arrived then terminate
```

Listing 5.4 Code skeleton for process depicted in Figure 5.7.

The process terminates when a signal (any data) arrives on input channel "zap" (Listing 5.4). But how does the sender know when there are no more data to process? Deadlock will occur if data arrive to be processed after the arrival of the termination signal. Worse, it may spread through the network according to data dependencies. The order in which processes may be terminated depends not just upon their interconnection, but upon the *history* of interaction between processes. Even if we introduce a globally connected "mother hen" process it will indeed be difficult to design so that it is always capable of deducing a valid order of termination.

Secure global termination #1: Exploiting data dependency

Advice regarding termination may be summarized, in decreasing preference, as follows.

1 Don't bother. Use non-terminating processes.
2 Add poison, exploiting data dependency.
3 Spread poison.

Systems may often be specified without the need for system termination. It is often included without due justification. However, if it is absolutely necessary then there are two approaches which guarantee security. One is obvious but not always applicable. The other is subtle but general.

Valid structure that guarantees correct termination forms part of the desired virtual communication architecture and should be implemented and tested *before* the addition of any system function. It should also be considered at an early phase of design.

When the process network is purely hierarchical, and thus free of any feedback, it is possible simply to add an extra component of protocol to every channel. This extra component is to carry *poison*. A process receiving poison first passes it on downstream, awaits an acknowledgement, then returns its own acknowledgement, and finally terminates. The acknowledgements (i.e. handshake synchronization) are not strictly necessary for secure termination. They allow the environment with which the system communicates to know when the entire system has terminated. If the application does not call for that then the handshake (i.e. returning of a "death certificate") may be safely omitted. In the experience of the author though, it often *is* a requirement. For example, the processors may be required to run another system, in which case some external operating system needs to know when they may be reallocated.

```
WHILE running
  up.in ? CASE
    food; data                  -- If data then
      ... process data          -- do something with them
    poison
      SEQ                       -- If poison then
        down.out ! poison       -- pass poison down pipe
        down.in ? death.certificate
        up.out ! death.certificate
        running := FALSE
```

Listing 5.5 Pseudocode for secure termination of a process within a bi-directional pipeline.

Such *variant protocol* is much like the concept of a variant record data structure. In fact the two are dual since a data structure just governs the protocol of asynchronous communication. Listing 5.5 illustrates how this might look in outline for a process within a pipeline[10].

Where the process replicated along the pipeline has been reduced to component processes, such as the farm worker discussed earlier (see Figure 5.3), a little thought will yield the modifications necessary, which follow the basic principle. The demultiplexor forwards the poison down the pipeline, and also to the worker process. It may then simply die. The worker subsequently need only poison the multiplexor and then die.

Once the multiplexor has received poison, it must then await the arrival of confirmation of the termination of the process further down the pipe. It then forwards confirmation of its own demise and terminates.

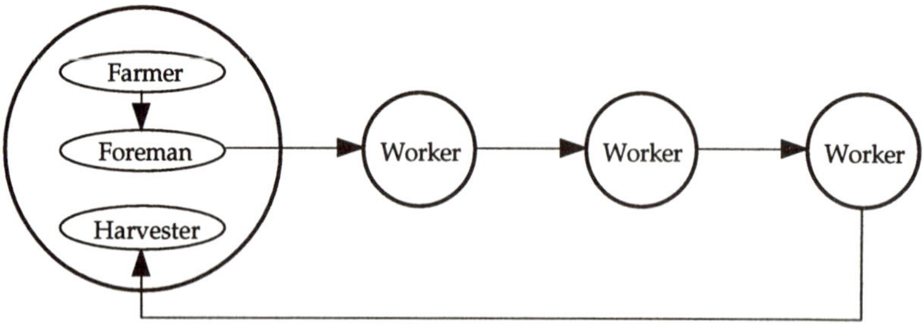

Figure 5.8 Farm implemented on a unidirectional ring interconnection network.

A simpler example of secure termination, by exploiting data dependency, may be found with a unidirectional pipeline. Figure 5.8 shows one implemented on a unidirectional *ring* interconnection network. The pseudocode of the required worker structure is given in Listing 5.6. The ring is used to implement a pipeline where, as with the other pipeline farm, considered earlier, the nature of the work distributed is independent of results received. Note that this is a new system, distinct and different from the earlier one. Each worker merely forwards work packets, if busy, and results packets, which are eventually harvested.

```
WHILE running
  SEQ
    up ? CASE
      work; work.pkt
        SEQ                     -- If work then
          ... conduct work      -- do it
          down ! results; results.pkt
      results; results.pkt      -- else forward results
        down ! results; results.pkt
      poison
        SEQ                     -- If poison then
          down ! poison         -- forward results
          running := FALSE      -- and terminate
```

Listing 5.6 Pseudocode for worker process in Figure 5.8.

In this example termination is initiated by the farmer. Poison propagates down the pipeline and eventually arrives at the harvester, causing the whole system to terminate securely.

In general, secure termination cannot always be achieved by exploiting data dependency because feedback may be present. Where feedback exists so does the possibility of the starvation of a process because a partner in communication has terminated prematurely.

Secure global termination #2: Spreading poison[11]

Surprisingly, an elegant algorithm exists which guarantees secure termination of *any* network of processes, regardless of the presence of feedback. It relies upon spreading poison down *all* output channels and not terminating until poison is received on *all* input channels. It may be regarded as the establishment of a higher-level protocol, that poison is to be the last item sent along *every* channel.

We begin by casting all processes into the form in Listing 5.7.

```
[N]CHAN OF MyProtocol in :-- N input channels
[M]CHAN OF MyProtocol out :-- M output channels
[N]BOOL live :            -- N flags for "i/p is live"
SEQ
  ... initialize        -- Make all input channels live
  ... process data      -- Perform function until poisoned
  ... finalize          -- Spread poison & "black hole" i/p
                        -- channels until each is poisoned
```

Listing 5.7 Outermost level of structure for each process able to spread poison.

Initialization comprises the assignment of flags to indicate that all input channels are "live", by which we mean that no poison has arrived on any of them. The subsequent fold contains code which inputs data, processes them, and outputs results. It does this until poison arrives on *any* input channel, whereupon that channel is recorded as dead. No more data will arrive upon such a channel. Note that more than one channel may be declared dead at this point because processing may have taken place in parallel.

```
-- {{{ finalize
PAR
  PAR i=0 FOR M              -- On each output channel
    out[i] ! poison          -- spread poison
  PAR i=0 FOR N              -- On each input channel,
    WHILE live[i]            -- while live,
      in[i] ? CASE
        food; any            -- "black hole" any data
          SKIP
        poison               -- until poison arrives
          live[i] := FALSE   -- then kill channel
-- }}}
```

Listing 5.8 Expansion of finalization fold in Listing 5.7.

Finalization comprises two tasks that are executed concurrently. Poison is spread onto all output channels, since none will be required further. At the same time, data arriving on every live input channel are accepted and then thrown away. It is as though that data are consumed by a "black hole" (Listing 5.8).

This algorithm guarantees that no process will terminate until every other process which sends it data does so. Thus no process will starve. However, data may be *lost* once termination is initiated.

Termination is just a special case of a broader requirement.

Secure global reset

Consider the following requirement.

➤ Following a signal from either environment or component process, every process in an arbitrary interconnection network is to be returned to a "reset" state.

  Data may be lost within the system between the issue of the reset signal and global completion of the reset. Further reset signals received within this time interval may thus cause no harm.

It turns out that the algorithm discussed previously can also be employed to effect a global reset. Instead of spreading poison we instead spread a reset signal. The only modification is to the required outermost level of component process structure, as shown in Listing 5.9.

```
[N]CHAN OF MyProtocol in :-- N input channels
[M]CHAN OF MyProtocol out :- M output channels
[N]BOOL live :              -- N flags for "i/p is live"
WHILE TRUE                  -- Non-terminating process
  SEQ
    ... initialize          -- Make all input channels live
    ... process data        -- Perform function until reset
    ... finalize            -- Spread reset, "black hole" i/p
                            -- channels until each is reset
```

Listing 5.9 Outermost level of structure for each process able to spread reset signal.

Remember, the last item any process sends along any channel is a reset signal. No data will arrive after a reset signal until the sender itself is reset. Globally, data may be lost after reset initiation until it has spread everywhere. Once the entire system has been reset it will once again be secure against data loss.

Global phenomena from purely local interaction

Finally, there is something philosophically significant about the algorithm described above.

There are fundamental differences between conventional artificial computation and the way nature achieves information processing.

- Natural computation is an emergent attribute of purely local interaction between a multitude of (often identical) parallel processes. Artificial computation is conventionally achieved via reductionism (functional decomposition). A small number of different processes interact globally.
- Nature *exploits* noise (errors or uncertainties) whereas conventional artificial computation excludes noise and is utterly intolerant of it.

It is believed by some that life, and perhaps even conscious self-awareness, may be global phenomena which emerge from the natural form of information processing.

Learning about computation from nature is arguably a good thing, especially regarding parallel processing which now offers probably the only way to maintain the continuous increase in performance that we have become accustomed to. Exploiting local, rather than global, interaction is the key to the parallel processing advantages of performance and scalability.

➤ The poison (or reset) spreading algorithm offers an elegant example of how to solve a problem in parallel processing without the need for global interaction. It achieves a global phenomenon with purely local interaction.

5.2 Granularity and scalability

5.2.1 Granularity

Degree of decomposition

Recall that, depending upon the application concerned, we may choose to regard "performance" in just two useful ways[12]. Note that both are issues of communication.

- Data throughput
- Event latency

Recall that instruction throughput is deemed not to be a useful measure as the amount of work done by each individual instruction varies between processors. However one may assess it, any processor has an upper limit to the performance of which it is capable. As a result, it is often desirable to divide the requirement across multiple processors. This, of course, is precisely the purpose of parallel processing.

Recall also that, in order to obtain the overall performance required, the load is divided and shared among multiple processors in either (or both) of the following ways[13].

- Domain decomposition
- Function decomposition

Granularity may be loosely defined as the degree to which decomposition is undertaken. With domain decomposition, the measure of granularity may be related to the inverse of the size of domain which remains undivided and encapsulated within each process. This is made even easier because a domain is constructed from atomic data which may thus be counted. For example, a graphics application which is implemented by domain decomposition all the way down to individual pixels (perhaps perceived as integers) has greater granularity than another which is only decomposed down to the level of (say) groups of 32 × 32 pixels. The latter implementation will be composed of roughly a thousand times fewer processes than the former.

Whilst it is just as easy *intuitively* to quantify granularity of function decomposition, it is not so easy to measure it formally. We might return to counting instructions executed in the evaluation of each function, but this suffers from the problem that some processors may achieve certain computations with fewer instructions than others. Worse, it is easy to be misled by counting instructions. Some evaluations might require fewer instructions with one processor than with another, but those instructions might take longer to execute than those of the competitor. There are only two solutions to the dilemma. One might establish a measure of function *grain size* which is only applicable to the processor type concerned. Alternatively, one might just count operations of a specific class, relevant to the application concerned, e.g. arithmetic operations in a numerical application.

Granularity defined independently of application

Such a loose definition of granularity is, unfortunately, an over-simplification. If there is one single message which might be distilled from this entire book it is the following.

➤ Computation is transformation and communication.
Communication is king over parallel system design.

Either measure of performance, responsiveness to events or data throughput, is a matter of communication. At each step, in decomposing the task to be performed, the amount of communication is increased. It is simply not possible to conduct task decomposition without increasing communication, regardless of the abstraction employed. It makes no difference whether we consider the system to be decomposed as a procedure, a function, or an object[14]. The results of decomposition must still communicate in order to compute.

➤ As the granularity of implementation increases, the ratio of transformation to communication of component processes decreases.

```
WHILE TRUE
  SEQ
    in ? datum                  -- Acquire next datum.
    ... compute result          -- Transform it.
    out ! result                -- Forward result.
```

Listing 5.10 Non-terminating data transform process.

Consider the process described by Listing 5.10. As long as a relevant definition of atomic computation is chosen, it is easy to relate the frequency of transformation to that of communication because the process is cyclic. We may choose to define an atomic communication either as one input or output, or as the sum of one input and one output. Life is just a little simpler if the sum is chosen.

➤ Consideration of the transformation/communication ratio allows a definition of granularity which is independent of decomposition and thus also of application.

It proves useful to define the grain size g as the ratio of transformation to communication.

$$g = f_t / f_c$$

f_t = frequency of atomic transformation
f_c = frequency of atomic communication

Granularity may now be thought of either intuitively, as the degree of decomposition, or as something measurable and independent of context, the reciprocal of grain size. The first possibility bears analogy with aggregates used in the construction of roads and buildings. Each grade of aggregate is the result of the decomposition of rock. Sand has much higher granularity (lower grain size) than gravel. The idea of aggregate granularity only serves comparison between degrees of decomposition. With software there exists a need to take account of the effect of decomposition upon the *nature* of the grains (processes) because it affects the way they interact with each other. That interaction consumes resources as does the scale of the computation.

Efficiency and scalability

As the degree of decomposition increases, less and less transformation, but more and more communication, per process is needed. Thus the demand per process on the resources available for transformation decreases while the demand for resources available for communication increases. The problem, if not already obvious, may be stated as follows.

➤ While the grain size of the hardware g_h remains a constant, defined by processor architecture, that of the software g_s depends upon the degree of decomposition.

The implication is that decomposition should attempt to forge a match between the granularity of the software and that of the hardware. Failure to do so will cause either under-utilization of transformation resources, or that of communication resources. Under-utilization implies inefficiency.

➤ Efficiency demands that the degree of decomposition should bring about a match between the grain size of software and hardware.

$$g_s \approx g_h$$

It may seem at first that this challenges scalability, but it is not necessarily so. Scalability of performance with hardware resources *may* be affected. To efficiently utilize *more* processors it will be necessary for them to possess reduced grain size in order to retain the match. To efficiently utilize *faster* processors[15] it will be necessary to ensure that they retain the same granularity in order to maintain the match.

➤ Scalability of performance with hardware resource requires either more processors with reduced grain size (and thus greater decomposition) or the same number of faster ones with granularity maintained (decomposition unchanged).

Scalability of *task* with hardware resource may also be affected, depending on the kind of decomposition performed. With domain decomposition, a greater domain may be processed with more of the same processes. As long as local communication dominates, software granularity will remain unchanged and thus more of the same processors may be utilized with efficiency maintained. However, the same is hard to achieve with function decomposition. The scale of task may then be forced to increase less rapidly than the number of processors.

➤ Scalability of domain with hardware resource is easily achieved via furthering domain decomposition and utilizing more processors of the same grain size.

5.2.2 Excess concurrency defeats latency

In any system which incorporates global communication the scalability of performance or task is going to be difficult to achieve, not just because the software granularity scales awkwardly but also because global message *latency*[16] will vary with the diameter of the interconnection network.

```
SEQ
  in ? data[0]                  -- Acquire first data
  ... compute result[0]         -- Compute first result
  in ? data[0]                  -- Acquire second data
  WHILE TRUE
    SEQ
      PAR
        in ? data[1]            -- Acquire next data
        ... compute result[1]   -- Compute next result
        out ! result[0]         -- Send previous result
      data[0], result[0] := data[1], result[1]
```

Listing 5.11 A process which cyclically evaluates a function and communicates globally.

Consider the form of process shown in Listing 5.11. It cyclically acquires data, computes the value of a function of those data, and outputs it, all without imposing any unnecessary order upon events. Once one result has been computed and one further data set has been input, and thus lies ready for processing, then there is no need to care about the order in which input, output, and processing next occur. Allowing communication and computation to interleave arbitrarily helps keep the processor busy.

➤ Good parallel design never imposes unnecessary event ordering.

If we count the sum of one input and one output as a single unit of communication then the process grain size g_s represents the number of computation steps per cycle. If we now choose to measure time in units equal to the time taken to perform a single computation step then we can more elegantly express an interesting conclusion.

Efficiency demands the following.

$$g_s > L$$

g_s = granularity of process
L = latency of interconnection network

To make this absolutely clear, consider a single cycle. If new data have not arrived and the previous result has not been accepted in the time taken to compute a result then the subordinate process described by the PAR construct cannot terminate. If Listing 5.11 describes the entire behaviour of a processor then that processor will be *idle* until the communication step has been completed. Idleness implies inefficiency. What can be done?

Over the entire system the rate of communication per computation may be assumed fixed by the decomposition. It is only the *delay* in communication (latency) that is causing the problem, not the rate at which it occurs. What is needed is a way of hiding that delay. Consider what happens if there are many more such processes than processors, as described by Listing 5.12.

```
PAR i=0 FOR N                              -- Replicate N of 'em
  SEQ
    in ? data[0]                           -- Acquire first data
    ... compute result[0]                  -- Compute 1st result
    in ? data[0]                           -- Acquire second data
    WHILE TRUE
      SEQ
        PAR
          in ? data[1]                     -- Acquire next data
          ... compute result[1]            -- Compute next result
          out ! result[0]                  -- Send last result
        data[0], result[0] := data[1], result[1]
```

Listing 5.12 Replication of a process which cyclically evaluates a function and communicates globally.

First note that software grain size g_s is unchanged. Communication and transformation occurring on a processor have increased in equal proportion. Only the amount of concurrency has changed.

Now, if new data have not arrived for an individual process once it has completed the evaluation of a new result then it may wait without leaving the processor idle provided that data have arrived for some other process. The processor need never be idle as long as the latency is less than the time taken to evaluate new results for *all* processes allocated to it.

Again, to make this clear, consider the initial behaviour. After computing the first result, the processor will be idle for a time L while it awaits the arrival of more data. But data for all processes allocated to the processor are in flight simultaneously. By the time the first evaluation is complete, data for a second process must have arrived. By the time that process has completed an evaluation, data for a third process must have arrived, and so on. However, the interval between data arriving for the same process is still equal to L units. This means that there must be enough processes allocated per processor to keep it busy computing for that long. In turn this means that there must be sufficient parallelism in the software to permit this.

➤ For a system which incorporates global communication decomposition must provide more processes than processors. The excess must be sufficient to hide the message latency imposed by the interconnection network employed.

A new relation expresses how the number of processes and their grain size depend upon the number of processors and the latency of their interconnection network. It follows from observing that the total time which a processor may spend computing, before latency implies idleness, is just the product of the number of processes per processor p/P and their grain size.

$$\frac{p}{P} \times g_s > L \qquad p = \textit{number of processes}$$

$$\Rightarrow \quad p \times g_s > P \times L \qquad P = \textit{number of processors}$$

This is an important relation which must be taken into account in the design of all parallel software. It is particularly important in its consequences for the design of systems in which global communication dominates and where latency is a function of interconnection network diameter. The maximum parallelism obtainable thus dictates a limit to scalability with the number of processors available.

5.2.3 Domain scaling and granularity

Scaling of volume to surface ratio

The last section spoke of a design constraint applicable where global communication dominates. Here, we examine the effect on granularity of domain scaling where local communication dominates.

First, forget all about computation for a while and just imagine a blob of ink on a piece of paper. If it is assumed to be roughly circular then a simple relation exists between the area and perimeter of the blob.

$$\textit{Perimeter} = \pi.d \qquad d = \textit{diameter}$$

$$\textit{Area} = \pi.d^2$$

$$\Rightarrow \quad \frac{\textit{Area}}{\textit{Perimeter}} \propto d$$

As the blob scales the ratio between the area and perimeter changes! In fact, the same principle holds regardless of the dimensionality of the domain. Imagine a blob of water spilled in a spaceship, where no gravity acts. It will form a (three-dimensional) sphere. The volume to surface ratio will depend upon the amount of water spilled.

$$\frac{V}{S} \propto d \qquad V = \textit{volume}$$

$$S = \textit{surface area}$$

It is impossible to imagine a blob of more than three dimensions since we cannot employ physical objects as analogies. However, anything whose value depends upon more than three independent variables has a form with more than three dimensions. The variation of the ratio of volume to surface area with scale is a principle that applies to objects with any number of dimensions. The relation above remains true regardless of dimensionality. The interpretation of the terms "volume" and surface" just needs to be extended to include their counterparts.

This observation tells us something very important. It is important both to our understanding of the world (our science) and our ability to make tools and objects (our technology and our engineering).

➤ When things change in size they usually also change in nature.

As an example, consider what happens as the size of a person scales. The human body generates heat roughly in proportion to its volume, by metabolism (chemical reactions which yield heat). It dissipates heat roughly in proportion to surface area, by sweating (evaporation which consumes heat). This is one reason why thin people find it easier to run up the stairs than do fat people, who have a much bigger volume to surface ratio. Even if they possess the same strength to weight ratio, fat people simply tend to overheat.

Granularity as a volume to surface ratio

In case the reader was beginning to wonder, the notion of a volume to surface ratio changing as something scales is deeply relevant to parallel processing. Volume may be considered an analogue of the transformation performed by a process and area to be one of communication. Granularity is now exposed as just another example of the idea of a volume to surface ratio.

Before the consequences of this are explored it will prove helpful to express the variation of volume to surface ratio in relation to volume rather than diameter. It is easiest to take the simplest case, i.e. that of dimensionality 2. Imagine the ink blob to be tessellated using tiles of unit area.

$$\frac{Area}{Perimeter} \propto \sqrt{Area}$$

This relation can be generalized to a space of dimensionality D as follows. Imagine an object to be made up of cells of unit volume which juxtapose so that there is no space vacant between them. If it requires n cells to fill up the object then the total volume is n units. It is possible to express the volume to surface ratio in terms of volume because volume is proportional to the diameter to the power D.

$$\frac{V}{S} \propto d, \quad V \propto d^D$$

$$\Rightarrow \quad \frac{V}{S} \propto V^{\frac{1}{D}}$$

The constant of proportionality depends solely upon the geometry of the blob. If it is a D-dimensional hypercube[17] (square in two dimensions, cubic in three dimensions) then it will possess $2D$ faces, each of $D - 1$ dimensions. Each edge will be of length equal to the Dth root of the volume. For example, each edge of a cube equals the cube root of its volume. Therefore, the exact expression of the volume to surface ratio for a hypercube form is as follows.

$$S = 2D\left(V^{\frac{1}{D}}\right)^{D-1}$$

$$\Rightarrow \quad \frac{V}{S} = \frac{V}{2D\left(V^{\frac{1}{D}}\right)^{D-1}} = \frac{V}{2DVV^{-\frac{1}{D}}}$$

$$\Rightarrow \quad \frac{V}{S} = \frac{1}{2D}V^{\frac{1}{D}}$$

Recall that volume is the analogue of computation. We had already concluded that granularity depends upon the degree of decomposition. This relation tells us *how* it will vary given domain decomposition. The relationship is clearly geometric and allows the determination of the limit to software scalability, which depends upon the dimensionality of the space of decomposition.

Example: granularity versus decomposition in two dimensions

Suppose it is possible to decompose the software into a square cellular array of identical processes which cyclically update their internal state and exchange state with their neighbours. If the state update requires c transformation steps then the grain size of a single process (Figure 5.9) is as follows.

$$g_s^{\min} = \frac{c}{4}$$

Having determined the finest possible software grain, it will be necessary to group a square array of them onto each processor. The number of processes per processor ($n = p/P$) should be chosen to achieve a match between software and hardware granularity, as discussed earlier.

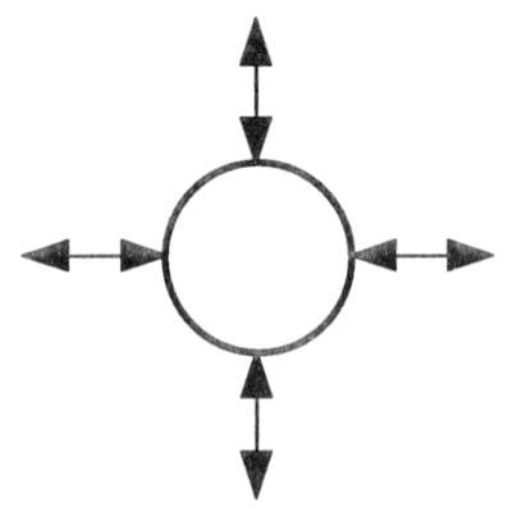

Figure 5.9 The smallest grain.

In order to calculate the new software grain size g_s it is necessary to know how many transformation time-steps are required to achieve a communication *internal* to the new composite process. For convenience, we shall assume here that an internal communication is equivalent to just one transformation time-step. g_s may now be expressed as follows.

$$g_s = \frac{nc + 4n - 4\sqrt{n}}{4\sqrt{n}} \qquad n = p/P = \textit{number of processes}$$

$$= \left(\frac{c}{4} + 1\right)\sqrt{n} - 1$$

$$= g_s^{\min}\sqrt{n}$$

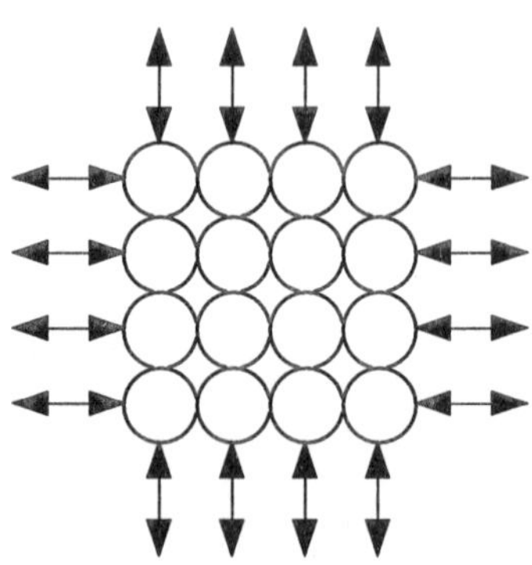

Figure 5.10 Aggregate of primitive processes to form composite grain.

For the sake of absolute clarity, there follows a summary of assumptions underlying this result.

- The number of atomic transformations per cycle and per unit domain is constant and equal to *c*.

- The number of atomic communications per cycle and per unit domain is constant and equal to 4.
- One atomic communication performed internally to a composite process requires the same time as just one atomic transformation.

Example continued: domain scaling with global communication

Consider the question of scalability if all communication in the example above were *global* and thus routed through an interconnection network with latency L. Such a system might effectively be the result of farming and domain decomposition. The farmer would encapsulate the entire domain but would repeatedly despatch a copy of each subdomain to one or other worker for processing. He would then use the results received from the worker concerned to update his "master copy". Suppose we have the following relation between latency L and size P, which would, for example, result from the use of a hypercube interconnection network.

$$L = K \log_2 P \qquad K = constant$$

Earlier, it was argued that excess parallelism, i.e. the use of more processes than processors, could hide the effects of interconnection network latency and so avoid any processor being idle awaiting communication. It was assumed then that granularity was purely additive. Afterwards, it was shown that the truth is a little more complicated for domain decomposition.

Given a toroidal decomposition, software granularity varies as the square root of the number of minimal processes combined together to describe the behaviour of any single processor. We need the transformation per communication available to the processor, i.e. the granularity at that level of decomposition, to exceed the delay in message transport, i.e. the latency.

$$g_s \approx g_s^{min}\sqrt{n} \approx k\sqrt{n} > L \qquad k = g_s^{min} = constant \qquad n = p/P$$

Suppose a small image is to be processed, say of 16×16 pixels. Table 5.1 shows that while decomposition onto 4 processors may be efficient, that onto 256 may well not be, depending upon the values for the constants k and K which apply.

Latency may be seen to increase rather slowly as the processor network is expanded. Unfortunately, because the same number of processes is spread over fewer and fewer processors, the granularity of the process that describes the behaviour of each processor falls rapidly. As a result, each processor will ultimately become idle while waiting either for new work or to forward the results of old work.

Table 5.1 Example of software decomposition versus size of processor network.

P	4	16	64	256
L	$2K$	$4K$	$6K$	$8K$
n	64	16	4	1
g_s	$8k$	$4k$	$2k$	k

It is possible, given the above relations, to quantify the excess parallelism required for a toroidal decomposition of processes to be efficiently executed on an interconnection network with latency that increases logarithmically with size, like the hypercube.

$$n > \left(\frac{K \log_2 P}{k} \right)^2$$

Should a design be required that calls for toroidal domain decomposition, but where execution is to be on a hypercube, then the above relation must hold or efficiency will suffer.

---

1 An abstraction is a model of an object which possesses only those features necessary in order for other objects to interact with it.

2 Window, Icon, Mouse, and Pointer.

3 One example of a very simple, but very useful, active object is a clock process that sends a timing signal at regular intervals.

4 Given synchronous communication, one can always implement *asynchronous* communication by inserting an appropriate buffer process.

5 As for any software system, individual component processes should be fully tested against their specification, as should the complete system.

6 See Chapter 6 for the definition and discussion of client/server protocol.

7 An alternative definition of client/server protocol might require the satisfaction of each request *before another is accepted*. Then deadlock could occur.

8 We have met the torus before, when considering interconnection networks. (See Chapter 5, Section 5.2.)

9 See Chapter 1, Section 1.1.

10 Channels pointing down the pipeline have two components, `food` and `poison`, carrying data and termination signal respectively. Those pointing up the pipeline have a component to carry results and one confirming imminent death. The active component is indicated upon each communication with a constant "tag" which precedes any associated data.

11 The algorithm described was invented by Professor Peter Welch of The University of Kent, Great Britain. P. H. Welch, *Graceful termination – graceful resetting*, proceedings of the 10th Technical Meeting of the Occam User Group (Amsterdam: IOS Press, 1989).

12 See Chapter 2, Section 2.1.

13 See Chapter 1, Section 1.1.

14 A process may be thought of as the *execution* of a procedure, the *evaluation* of a function or the *activity* of an object.

15 It is assumed that this means the ability to execute more of the *same* instructions per unit time.

16 Message latency is defined as the delay between transmission and reception.

17 See Chapter 4, Section 4.3.

Chapter 6

Deadlock Avoidance

6.1 Abstraction of system, behaviour, and program

6.1.1 System

The object metaphor for software structure is often presented as an extension to that of the procedure, whose atom is state update. To this is added synchronous communication. Each object is defined by the messages it understands and its responses to them. Such responses are made up of updates of encapsulated (private) state and the sending of further messages to other objects. Both state update and synchronous communication may be unified in the abstract notion of an *event*.

One of the reasons for the great success of the object metaphor for software may well be that it is similar to the way in which we humans abstract the world around us[1]. Each object we encounter is represented in two ways: first, according to its *interaction* with other objects; secondly, according to its *classification*. The set of other objects with which interaction occurs decides the context of abstraction. Interaction attributes allow us to predict the behaviour of the object in that context. Classification attributes render use of the object metaphor efficient and manageable. Here, as is the case throughout this book, we are solely concerned with interaction.

Each possible behaviour of an object is referred to as a "process". Every process has an *alphabet* of events which may occur when it runs. To be more precise, a process alphabet is a set of event *classes*. For example, a telephone is capable of ringing. Each time it rings we may say that an *instance* of the event class "ring" from the alphabet of the object class known as "telephone" has occurred. The alphabet of a process P is denoted by αP. A parallel composition of processes forms a collective process whose alphabet is the union of all component process alphabets.

$$\Psi = \|_{i=1}^{N} P_i \qquad (1 \le i \le N)$$
$$\Rightarrow \alpha\Psi = \bigcup_{i=1}^{N} \alpha P_i$$

Any interaction between objects may be represented by a *shared event* which requires co-operation between the processes concerned. For example, a printer must interact with a sheet-feeder in order to print a page. This may be regarded as a single shared event in which both sheet-feeder and printer participate. Such interaction may be thought of as synchronous communication where the page passed is the message. Synchronization must be achieved for any shared event to occur. In the case of the printer and sheet-feeder this might be brought about by gears meshing.

Events may, in theory, be shared between any number of processes. However, any such co-operation may equally be achieved by a number of *binary* interactions. Hence, it is sufficient to consider compositions where no event is shared by more than two processes. Such a system is referred to as *triple disjoint*.

$$\forall \{i, j, k\}, i \ne j \ne k . \alpha P_i \cap \alpha P_j \cap \alpha P_k = \varnothing$$

There is not much point in considering systems where some processes are known a priori to be faulty, so we assume that no component process is itself capable of progressing to a state where it refuses to participate in *any* interaction. A system where all component processes are themselves free of deadlock is referred to as *busy*. Any process which refuses to interact, but which is instead engaged in an infinite sequence of internal events, is said to *diverge* from desired behaviour. Systems of interest are those which are busy and composed of divergence-free processes.

It is useful to draw a distinction between interaction (sharing an event) and communication (passing a message). Communication has an associated *direction*, that of data flow. This is not relevant to the study of deadlock, where only synchronization is important. Hence, two distinct graphs may be defined which represent interaction and communication respectively. The *interaction graph* of a system possesses a node to represent each and every component process and an edge[2] to represent each shared event. There may therefore exist more than one edge between any two nodes. The corresponding *communication graph* is identical except that each edge is replaced with an arc in order to represent the direction of data flow. It thus forms a directed graph. In either graph, each edge (arc) may be labelled with the symbol denoting the relevant shared event. Remember that such an event may occur on more than one occasion, as multiple instances of common class. It may help to think of the edge (arc) as representing a channel which permits the necessary synchronization.

In order to consider the possibility of deadlock it is only necessary to consider interaction. All other events may be ignored. The set of events which capture interaction within a system is referred to as its *vocabulary* (denoted by Λ). It may be defined as the union of all intersections between component process alphabets.

$$\Lambda = \bigcup \{ \alpha P_i \cap \alpha P_j | i \neq j \}$$

We are interested in systems where at least one component process alphabet includes events which constitute interaction with their *environment*. We must be careful to take such events into account, in addition to the system vocabulary.

6.1.2 Behaviour

It is reasonable to assume that all systems begin activity at some point, in other words, that it is possible to find an instance of some event which may be observed first. We might think of this as the first thing we may record after switching on. No such assumption need be made regarding an ending. We shall be prepared for the possibility that a process might run for ever.

Imagine being an observer. Each time an event occurs it may be recorded. The sequence of events so recorded is called a *trace*[3]. The term usually refers to the sequence of events observed, up to some given point, from system start. It is thus never complete unless *termination* is explicitly included. A special symbol may be appended to indicate that termination has occurred.

It is necessary to go beyond the event history in order to characterize the *state* of a system. Following a given trace, each process is unlikely to be equally willing to engage in any event chosen from its alphabet. The set of events in which process P_i refuses to participate is denoted by X_i and is incorporated into the definition of system state. It is not necessarily true that the refusal set of a process is predictable given the trace. The *refusal set* (Ξ) of the entire system is just the union of those of all component processes. To summarize, system state is defined to be the combination of trace and refusal set.

$$\sigma = [s, \underline{X}] \qquad s = \langle e_1, e_2, e_3, \ldots, e_m \rangle$$

$$\Xi = \bigcup_{i=1}^{N} X_i \qquad \underline{X} = \{ X_i | 1 \leq i \leq N \}$$

When one process becomes ready to participate in a shared event it makes a *request* of the other for synchronization. If the other is not ready then the request is said to be *ungranted*. Whether or not a request is made or granted depends upon system state. Ungranted requests are of particular interest to the study of deadlock when neither participant is ready to engage in any event outside the system vocabulary, including any interaction with the environment. Such requests are then said to be ungranted *with respect to the vocabulary*. Note that the requesting process might still be successful with some other partner and thus be able to proceed. There follows an example of notation, and set-theoretic definition.

$$(\alpha P_i - X_i) \cap \alpha P_j \neq \varnothing \qquad \textit{Make request } (i \neq j)$$

$$\alpha P_i \cap \alpha P_j \subseteq X_i \cup X_j \qquad \textit{Request ungranted}$$

$$(\alpha P_i - X_i) \cup (\alpha P_j - X_j) \subseteq \Lambda \qquad \textit{with respect to vocabulary}$$

$$\Leftrightarrow \qquad P_i \xrightarrow{\sigma,\Lambda} \bullet P_j$$

The above expression asserts that a request of one process to participate in an event shared with another will go ungranted, at a particular state of the system, and when neither process can participate in any event outside the vocabulary. This is a notion which is actually quite simple, even though it requires a complicated verbal explanation. The mathematical notation makes it much easier to reason with.

The theory of Communicating Sequential Processes (CSP) uses set theory to permit a precise definition of these ideas. First, it must be appreciated that the state describes the system *between* two events occurring. To assert that P_i makes a request of P_j means that there is at least one event in the alphabet of P_j that is shared by P_i, and in which P_i is ready to participate. Whether or not the request is granted is decided by whether it lies outside or within the set of events in which either process refuses to participate. Consideration is restricted to when both participants are willing only to engage in events from the system vocabulary. This is sufficient because internal events may all occur without affecting the possibility of deadlock, and because we assume that the environment is well behaved and does not starve the system.

Conflict is said to occur between a pair of processes if both are ready to engage in a shared event but *cannot agree on which one*. A system in which no pair of processes ever conflict is said to be conflict free and satisfies the following predicate.

$$\forall \sigma \neg \exists \{i, j\}, i \neq j. \left(P_i \xrightarrow{\sigma,\Lambda} \bullet P_j\right) \wedge \left(P_j \xrightarrow{\sigma,\Lambda} \bullet P_i\right)$$

In words, at any state of the system there must be no pair of processes which are both ready to interact, but which refuse each other's request. It is possible to separate this concern as one of local protocol. It may, at first, appear that conflict freedom is required in order to guarantee deadlock freedom. However, this is not the case. It is possible for a system to encounter states where conflicts occur without deadlock being the result. On the other hand, design begins with a high level of abstraction. It is desirable that such an abstraction should represent interaction between any pair of processes as a single class of event and so allow no possibility of conflict.

At any system state, processes make requests of each other which may or may not be granted. The interaction graph captures the interdependence of processes with regard to system vocabulary but without regard to system state. In order to capture success or failure at synchronization we construct the *synchronization graph*. Such a graph may be constructed for each system state. A node represents each and every process. An arc represents each request, and is oriented towards the process of which the request is made. Each granted request may be identified as a *rotation*[4] in the synchronization graph. Conflict freedom guarantees that both arcs of a rotation represent the same event, which may then occur.

6.1.3 Program

The aim of studying parallel processing is to learn how to design and construct parallel systems which are valid, efficient, and scalable. In this chapter our concern is validity. We primarily wish to learn how to *design* valid systems. By "design" we mean the decomposition of a system into components, each of which has a precisely specified interface. In a valid design all interfaces are consistent, both with each other and with the desired system behaviour. It is the purpose of a program both to describe fully the decomposition, including all interfaces, and to implement all components. It is useful to render these two functions distinct in order to separate the concerns of design and implementation.

So far, we have shown how a system, and its behaviour, may be represented with mathematical precision. It is highly desirable that we may be able to represent a program too with the same precision.

A first step in design is to specify component processes as alphabets, and then construct their interaction graph. In order to complete the design, it remains to compose a protocol to *constrain the order in which events may occur*. Such a protocol forms part of a parallel design and is critical to program validity.

There is a fundamental reason why the composition of valid parallel programs is difficult. Any program which guarantees consistent event ordering must incorporate a *global* protocol for interaction. However, the whole purpose of design is to reduce the scope of concern, to divide and conquer. We thus seek *local* protocols. Problems such as divergence and deadlock are *holistic* whereas design is typically *reductionist*. Yet, if we abandon reductionism then how may we manage a project and divide workload? Fear not, reductionist design need not be abandoned, as we shall see later in this chapter. Certain purely local protocols may guarantee valid global protocol.

Component processes may be abstracted as alphabets which hide all internal events. Events may initially be enumerated according to the alphabet to which they belong. Given the hiding, most will be shared and thus be members of the system vocabulary. The remainder represent interaction with the system environment.

One possible convention for event notation is as follows.

$$\alpha P_i = \left\{e_1^i, e_2^i, \ldots, e_m^i, \ldots\right\}$$

$$\alpha\Psi = \left\{e_{m,n}^{i,j} = e_m^i = e_n^j, \ldots\right\}$$

Events which make up the system vocabulary and interaction with the environment must be isolated and enumerated prior to the determination of a valid global protocol.

Recall that, in the previous chapter, it was concluded that good parallel design never imposes unnecessary event ordering. Determination of the minimum necessary amount is made easier by employing a programming language which permits a varying degree of constraint. Thus the traditional procedure metaphor and structured programming would seem too harsh a mistress. Rather than introduce freedom into programs which are totally constrained by default, we should approach parallel programming as the gradual introduction of constraint into programs which are *totally unconstrained* by default.

A global protocol may be expressed by a strict partial order of events. A strict partial order is the combination of a set and a relation which is both non-reflexive and transitive.

$$\xi = \left(\left\{x_i \middle| 1 \le i \le n\right\}, \sim\right) \qquad \textit{A strict partial order is}$$

$$\left(x_i \sim x_j\right) \Rightarrow \neg\left(x_j \sim x_i\right) \qquad \textit{non-reflexive}$$

$$\left(x_i \sim x_j\right) \wedge \left(x_j \sim x_k\right) \Rightarrow \left(x_i \sim x_k\right) \qquad \textit{and transitive}$$

A strict partial order might be determined, on the system vocabulary, to express a minimum global protocol which guarantees valid behaviour.

$$o(\Psi) = [\Lambda, \triangleright]$$

Given the global protocol, we should be able to deduce the local protocol which would form part of the interface definition of each process. Unfortunately, for any real system this is likely to be just too difficult for the reason given earlier. It requires consideration of the entire system at once, holistically. Also, no obvious method for derivation presents itself, other than trial and error. Clearly, what is needed is a set of local *design rules* which *produce* valid protocol. We need a priori design, rather than a posteriori analysis. Such rules will govern local event ordering, which might also be expressed as a strict partial order.

$$o(P_i) = [\gamma P_i, \triangleright] \qquad \gamma P_i = \alpha P_i \cap \Lambda$$

Security requires support from the tools employed to design and compose programs. An ideal formal programming language might offer a unique and valid meaning to every program, and the reverse, a unique program to determine each correct behaviour. The former is desirable because the legality of a statement in a given programming language can be checked by automation, which would then guarantee a valid program and thus correct behaviour. The latter is desirable because the fewer ways there are of expressing a single behaviour the more openly readable and portable are programs. Such an ideal language does not yet exist, and perhaps never will. However, CSP and occam at least rest on solid formal foundations. It is important to appreciate that security does depend on the quality of the tools used, as well as the skill of the engineer. In this sense, software is just the same as cars or bridges, on which our safety regularly depends. Let us all hope that the best available tools are also the ones which get used.

6.2 Deadlock

6.2.1 Definition

In order to approach a precise definition of deadlock let us consider the interaction between a system, with process P, and its environment. We abstract the process solely in accordance with that interaction and thus define its alphabet αP. Any such process has an associated set of events P^0 in which it may participate first. Its environment will similarly define a set of events X which it offers the system when it starts. If it is possible that interaction may fail to commence then X is said to be a *refusal* of P. The set of refusals is a characteristic of any given process.

Should there be any events offered by the environment in which the process is ready to participate, we might hope that one of them will occur so that interaction begins. However, it is not necessarily so. The process may refuse to co-operate. Even though it is free to participate in a shared event, it may decide not to. Any process which *guarantees* to co-operate is referred to as *deterministic* because its behaviour is determined by the environment, according to the set of events offered. Determinism may thus be defined as guaranteed co-operation with a reasonable environment. The only refusals of a deterministic process are those sets of events offered which contain no event in which it may initially participate.

$$X \in \mathit{refusals}(P) \Leftrightarrow X \cap P^0 = \varnothing \qquad \textit{Determinism}$$

This is sufficient to define determinism, but not to define a deterministic process. Such a process *always* co-operates with its environment. *(P/s)* denotes the process *P* after trace *s* has been recorded. A deterministic process is one which remains deterministic after every trace which it is capable of causing. A process that is unable to guarantee determinism at all times is said to be non-deterministic. Interaction with such a process is much more likely to end in deadlock.

Suppose the environment offers the set of events *X* after trace *s* and the system process refuses to participate in any of them. *X* is thus a refusal of *(P/s)*. The combination of trace and refusal is referred to as a *failure* of the system because deadlock will ensue. The set of failures is a more general characteristic of a process since it incorporates refusals (those failures which follow a null (empty) trace). It constitutes a relation between past and imminent behaviour.

$$\mathit{failures}(P) = \{(s, X) \mid s \in \mathit{traces}(P), X \in \mathit{refusals}(P/s)\}$$

Remember that a failure may exist either because the environment fails to co-operate by offering only inappropriate events, or because the system fails to co-operate by behaving non-deterministically.

Any failure describes a deadlock. Such deadlock is not quite the focus of our interest because at least some of the blame may lie with the environment. The situation is much more worrying when the system refuses *all* events that it shares with its environment. We then say that the system itself has deadlocked and can state precisely what we mean by the deadlock freedom of a system.

$$\neg \exists s \in \mathit{traces}(P).(s, \alpha P) \in \mathit{failures}(P)$$

To declare a system deadlock free we require that *no* trace exists after which it refuses all interaction. Since we are unlikely to know the set of traces in advance, it is more useful to deny any imaginable sequence of events from the alphabet.

$$\neg\exists s \in (\alpha P)^{*}.(s, \alpha P) \in failures(P)$$

$(\alpha P)^{*}$ = *set of all possible finite sequences of events from* αP

One possible reason why such a failure might be observed would be a *divergence* of the system. A divergence of a process is a trace following which it refuses to engage in any interaction, despite unceasing internal activity. The only possible divergences of the systems considered so far would be caused by *livelock*, where component processes are engaged in an eternal cycle of internal interactions. This is because we have previously declared all component processes divergence free. Livelock remains a threat to system validity, but we do not consider it here. All system abstractions considered are busy and divergence free. At a sufficiently high level of abstraction they will also be conflict free.

The behaviour of any system may be defined by an outside observer as a process with the following three attributes.

- An alphabet αP
- A set of divergences *divergences(P)*
- A set of failures *failures(P)*

Any combination of divergence and subsequent refusal constitutes a failure, which explains why it is necessary to consider only divergence-free systems with regard to deadlock. Only then are we afforded the above definition of deadlock freedom and the conclusion that any perceived deadlock of the system corresponds to deadlock internal to it.

Now that we have stated precisely both the systems and the observed behaviour which are of interest, we are ready to investigate internal deadlock states.

6.2.2 Deadlock states

By system deadlock we mean that the system refuses to engage in *any* event whatsoever, including the vocabulary, interaction with the environment, and events internal to component processes. For every trace which contradicts the condition for deadlock freedom there exists a corresponding *deadlock state* which may be represented by an appropriate synchronization graph.

A process is said to be *blocked* when it is ready to interact with at least one partner but no such partner is itself ready. It is thus quite unable to proceed. Blocking may be defined more precisely in terms of ungranted requests. The following conditions assert that process P_i is blocked.

$$\exists j.P_i \xrightarrow{\sigma} P_j \qquad\qquad P_i \textit{ makes some request}$$

$$\forall j.\left(P_i \xrightarrow{\sigma} P_j\right) \Rightarrow \left(P_i \xrightarrow{\sigma,\Lambda} \bullet P_j\right) \qquad\qquad \textit{All its requests are blocked}$$

Given that each component process is itself free of both deadlock and divergence, it follows that, in a deadlock state, *all* are blocked. A consequence of this is as follows.

➤ For any system which is free of conflict, the synchronization graph of any deadlock state contains no rotations.

All component processes will subsequently suffer starvation because it is impossible for any process to cease to be blocked. After a little thought one might surmise that the cause of this state of affairs is that they are starving each other[5]. In that one would be correct. One might further surmise that cycles of ungranted requests exist in the synchronization graph. Again, one would be correct. However, one would be quite wrong to conclude that any such cycle *implies* deadlock, as Figure 6.1 illustrates. It requires a little more than that.

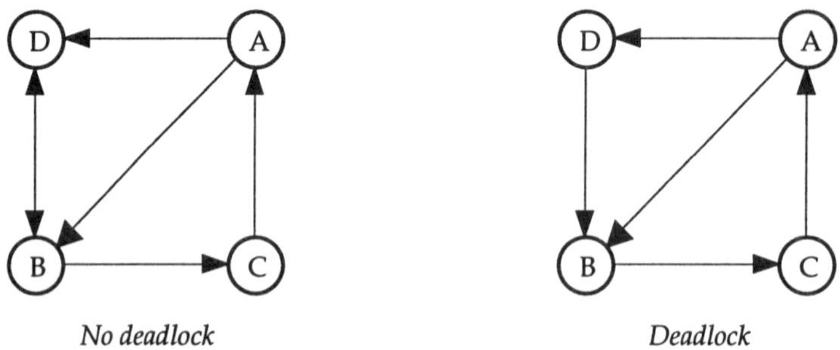

Figure 6.1 Cycles of ungranted requests and deadlock.

Figure 6.1 shows two possible states of a system depicted by their synchronization graph. The one on the left is able to proceed because B is not blocked and is thus able to satisfy the request from D, which may then satisfy A, and thus break the cycle of ungranted requests $\langle A, B, C\rangle$. The cycle, however, remains a *symptom* of deadlock.

➤ The synchronization graph of any deadlock state of a busy, triple-disjoint system contains at least one cycle of ungranted requests.

The synchronization graph on the right of Figure 6.1 depicts deadlock. All processes are blocked. There is thus no process remaining which is free to begin a chain of granted requests.

6.3 Deadlock avoidance by design

6.3.1 Consistent event ordering

Consider a set of processes which lie on a circuit[6] in the interaction graph of a system (Fig. 6.2). Suppose each one interacts just once with each neighbour and then terminates. Interactions obey a clockwise order beginning at "noon". A corresponding cycle of ungranted requests in the synchronization graph will inevitably result. The *local* protocols combine to produce an invalid *global* protocol. However, it would only require one process to break ranks to remove the problem.

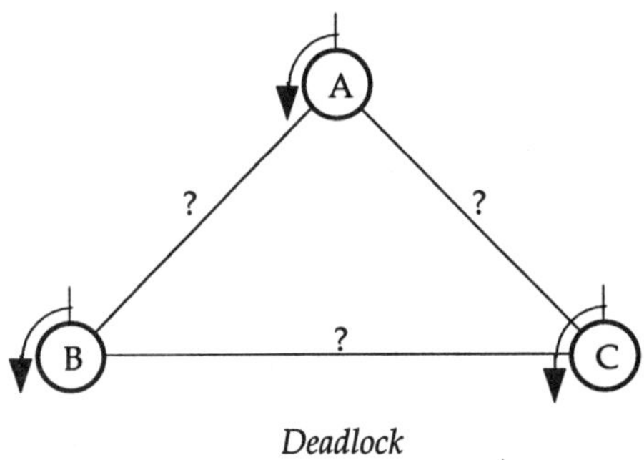

Figure 6.2 Inconsistent event ordering.

Intuition alone affords such conclusions. It would not be so easy with a more complicated system. A more generally applicable method is to seek an *edge labelling* of the interaction graph that is consistent with all local protocols. Such a modified graph would represent consistent event ordering, and thus a valid global protocol. It would be sufficient to prove the system deadlock free because at least one process would always be free to proceed. Figure 6.3 shows the modified interaction graph for the system described above. Note that starvation of any single process is also impossible.

A zero from which one can always graduate is the case where no process in a cycle cares about the ordering of its interactions. Any ordering of events is then possible, so it requires no effort to find one. If we define the local protocol as a strict partial order then this class of process is represented by one which is *empty*.

It might appear that such an approach represents a posteriori analysis (trial and error) rather than a priori design, but it is not necessarily so. Having reduced the system required to a number of component processes and their interaction, a designer may then establish local protocols which are known a priori to combine to produce valid global protocol. The purpose of design is thus fulfilled. Each component process may subsequently be separately designed or implemented according to an adequately specified interface.

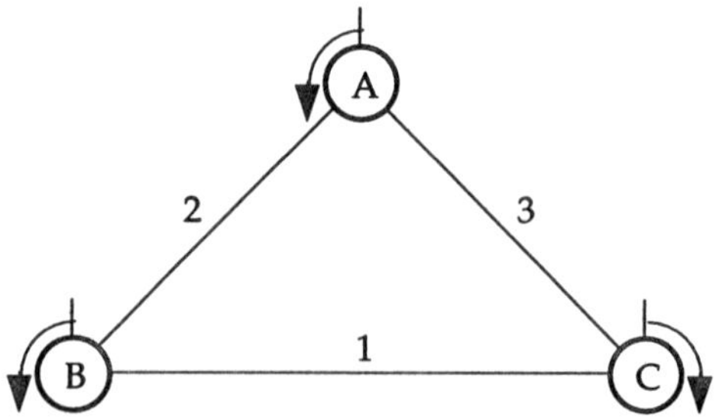

Figure 6.3 Consistent event ordering, shown by labelling edges of interaction graph.

We now turn to examine some such local protocols.

6.3.2 Cyclic order protocol

A certain class of process suggests itself, following the previous discussion.

➤ A Cyclic Ordered Process is iterative and guarantees interaction with each of its neighbours exactly once each cycle according to a strict partial order.

It cannot be overemphasized here that such a process serves only as an *abstraction* of the real one. Such an abstraction captures the features that are salient to the design of a valid virtual communication architecture. Each event shared with a neighbour serves to represent *any* interaction. More detailed design may follow later subject to the condition that it offers a valid refinement of the current one.

Imagine a system entirely composed of cyclic ordered processes. Each one may be different and may obey a distinct strict partial order. Either all are non-terminating or all must agree on the number of iterations to perform.

If they were all of the same zero class, such that the defining strict partial order were empty, then deadlock could never occur. Globally, events may occur in any order without breaching local protocol. This represents a generalization of the example discussed earlier, which might now be regarded as cyclic, but with just one iteration.

Synchronous communication between two processes constitutes an event shared between the two processes and which is synchronized when an input in one and the corresponding output in the other are both ready. A process which conducts all its inputs and outputs in parallel exactly once per cycle is referred to as *I/O PAR*. Any system composed entirely of I/O PAR processes can never deadlock because it may be characterized by an empty strict partial order of interaction events. Listing 6.1 shows a process which is I/O PAR.

```
SEQ
  ... initialization
  WHILE running
    SEQ
      PAR
        PAR i=0 FOR number.of.input.channels
          ... i'th input
        PAR j=0 FOR number.of.output.channels
          ... j'th output
      ... computation
```

Listing 6.1 An I/O PAR process.

Consider systems composed entirely of non-zero cyclic ordered processes which have circuits in their interaction graph. Remember that each process makes just one request at any time. For any such circuit, it is possible that, at some point in time, requests may form a closed trail[7], in which case deadlock ensues. Worse, if any request goes ungranted in any single cycle then it will *never* subsequently be granted. Because of the cyclic nature of each process, if all requests of every process are granted in the first cycle then they always will be.

It is therefore sufficient to concentrate on a single cycle of such a system in order to discover how component processes may be connected to produce valid global protocol. Recall that such protocol comprises a global strict partial order of interactions.

➤ Any system composed only of cyclic ordered processes is free of deadlock if, and only if, there exists no closed trail of dependent events in the interaction graph.

One interaction is said to depend upon another if it occurs earlier in the global strict partial order created by connecting processes. Because only one interaction can take place per cycle between any connected pair of processes, the notion of dependency may be extended to channels. As a result the same basic method of consistent edge labelling may be employed as used earlier with acyclic ordered processes. It is *constructive*, as is required of a design method. One can imagine a tool which denies the designer the ability to construct a design incorrectly.

```
SEQ
  ... initialization
  WHILE running
    SEQ
      PAR i=0 FOR number.of.input.channels
        ... i'th input
      ... computation
      PAR j=0 FOR number.of.output.channels
        ... j'th output
```

Listing 6.2 An I/O SEQ process.

A non-zero class of Cyclic Ordered Process is one where, upon each cycle, all inputs are performed in parallel *prior* to the performance of all outputs in parallel. Such a process is called *I/O SEQ* and is illustrated in Listing 6.2. A consequence of the above rule for deadlock freedom is that a network of I/O SEQ processes will never deadlock provided that there is no directed circuit in the communication graph. Note that the direction of data flow has now become important to the consideration of deadlock, but only because it is associated with a constraint upon event ordering. Note also that the program implies a greater constraint upon event ordering than that of the I/O PAR process in Listing 6.1, even though it appears no more complicated.

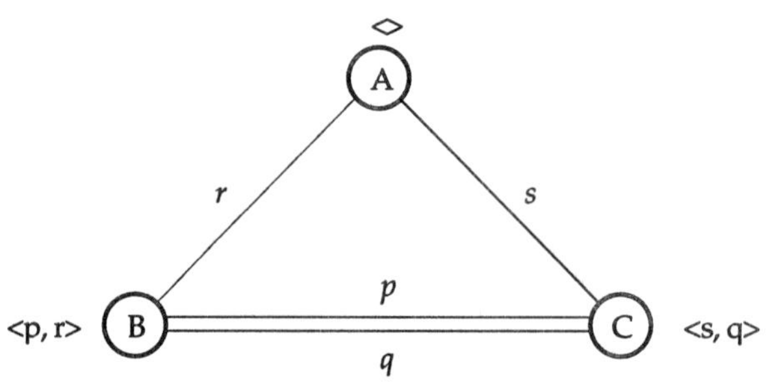

Figure 6.4 Cyclic Ordered Process interaction graph, refined to include a choice.

Perhaps the first way in which we might wish to refine our design is to reduce the degree of abstraction of process interaction. Instead of employing a single event to represent interaction between a pair of processes, we might distinguish two distinct possibilities. Figure 6.4 represents such a system. It might at first appear that interaction between *B* and C should be required to be conflict free. After all, if they are ready to interact but cannot agree on precisely how to do so then how can the design be secure against deadlock? In fact, if the above constraint applies, as it does in the system depicted, then all conflicts are transient. Deadlock can never occur.

```
-- A                -- B              -- C
PAR                 PAR               PAR
  ... r               ... q             ... p
  ... s               SEQ               SEQ
                        ... p             ... s
                        ... r             ... q
```

Listing 6.3 Program structure inferring the partial order of events of each process in Figure 6.4.

Listing 6.3 shows the program structure which would give rise to the partial order of events which describe each process in Figure 6.4. Note that, although a choice of event exists in the interaction of *B* and *C*, no selection of behaviour is included in any program.

Before we get carried away thinking that we now know how to design any required parallel system to be deadlock free, let us consider the limitations of cyclic ordered processes. Anyone schooled in structured programming should immediately recognize the absence of one primary behavioural form. There is no *selection*. Such processes are utterly unable to modify their interactive behaviour according to their history, as recorded by updating internal state.

We need to be precise about what we mean by "selection". For example, consider a person interacting with a vending machine. Such a machine typically offers its customers a choice of items. An *external choice* is made. The system process is said to be deterministic in this regard because its environment determines behaviour. However, now consider the giving of change. If the degree of abstraction required demands that we care *which* coins are returned then the process must be regarded as non-deterministic. This is because an *internal choice* may be made by the machine. Customers can neither control nor tell how their change will be dispensed.

Perhaps the coins returned mattered because the customer needed a particular coin to make a phone call. On the other hand, if the choice of coins makes no difference to the pattern of future interaction then it should be disregarded in the abstraction employed for design. A unique event should be employed which just represents the giving of change, regardless of *how* it is given. Non-deterministic selection is undesirable in design abstraction. We all find it difficult enough to deal with uncooperative behaviour in our daily lives. There is no reason to build it into our automation.

Cyclic ordered processes are sufficient as an abstraction to enable the valid design of systems which interact without regard to the history of that interaction. They are well suited to many applications, often those derived by domain decomposition. More complicated abstractions are needed to guarantee validity where component processes incorporate selection.

6.3.3 Client/server protocol

Shallow abstraction: unique shared events

Cyclic ordered processes are fine for design by pure domain decomposition and where local interaction between processes follows a fixed pattern. However, many applications require a design which includes processes whose behaviour depends upon the history of interaction with their neighbours. Such processes frequently remain cyclic, but the order in which they interact with their neighbours, upon any particular cycle, depends upon events which have already occurred. A cashpoint machine may not follow a request by dispensing cash, but instead signal its masters that it needs a refill. A file manager may refuse a request for write access to a particular file because an earlier such request was granted and it remains claimed. In both of these examples a *client* is starved of the desired response and may in turn cause starvation for any other process to whom it acted as *server*, and so on recursively.

There is one way in which cyclic processes may be safely combined when the order of their shared events is *not* fixed in advance at design-time. It forms a second example of a purely *local* protocol between combined cyclic processes which may be shown to guarantee valid global protocol. Once again, attention is restricted to busy, triple-disjoint systems composed of divergence-free processes.

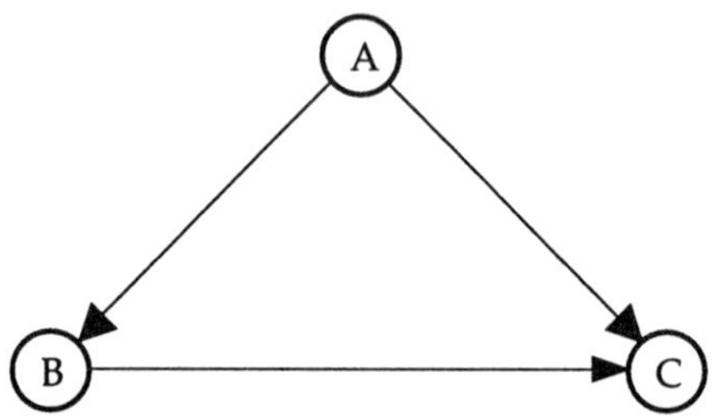

Figure 6.5 Directed interaction graph showing simple client/server protocol.

Design is represented (at any given level of abstraction) as a *directed interaction graph*. The orientation of each arc has nothing to do with the direction of data flow. Instead it indicates a reliable dependency, usually referred to as a *client/server protocol*. Figure 6.5 shows that *A* acts as client to both *B* and *C*, and that *B* acts as client to *C*.

CS1 A server guarantees to grant a request from a client unless awaiting the grant of a request it has itself made as client to another server.

Clearly, one cannot label any process as either server or client. A client/server protocol merely establishes a *relation* between a pair of processes. A directed interaction graph, such as that depicted in Figure 6.5, should not be confused with a synchronization graph, which is bound to a particular system state, or with a communication graph, which represents data flow. Clients do not necessarily become ready to engage in (make a request for) the shared event first, though that may often be the case. Each arc represents a unique event shared between the processes at either end and means that condition CS1 is true for that event. Note that the unique shared event typically abstracts many different events which are distinct at a deeper level of abstraction. For example, it might not distinguish the *value* of a datum communicated.

Any system of which Figure 6.5 represents a valid abstraction is free of the possibility of deadlock. This conclusion is only possible because a second condition is true for the interaction graph considered as a whole.

CS2 Any system which may be represented by a directed interaction graph which is free of any circuit is itself free of deadlock.

Should a directed circuit of client/server protocols exist then it becomes possible for any process upon it to suffer a permanently ungranted request from its server (the next process on the trail). It is thus possible for *all* processes to starve giving rise to deadlock. Note, however, that this is only *possible*, not certain, because the directed interaction graph only represents interactions which *may* take place. It says nothing of what *will* take place. It thus offers a rather high level of abstraction which is perhaps remote from reality. Although it places a strong constraint upon design, the guarantee of deadlock freedom it offers may find broader application than that acquired through the use of processes with a fixed pattern of interaction.

It is interesting to notice that a trail of client/server protocol interactions amounts to *recursive* service. In order to provide service at the top of the hierarchy, a server must act as client to one lower down, and so on. Condition CS2 amounts to a requirement of termination of such recursion.

Deep abstraction: multiple shared events

Abstracting interaction between two processes as a unique shared event class is fine provided that the pattern of interaction does not depend on the particular event that occurs at any time. If a unique shared event abstracts the communication of data then the subsequent behaviour of either process, with regard to its neighbours, must not depend upon, for example, which channel it arrived upon (if more than one exists), the identity of the data (its data type and meaning), or upon the value of those data. In other words, there can be no *selection* involved. If we wish to allow selection between behaviours then we must reduce the level of abstraction and distinguish between multiple event classes. Each class may represent a distinct channel, variable, or value.

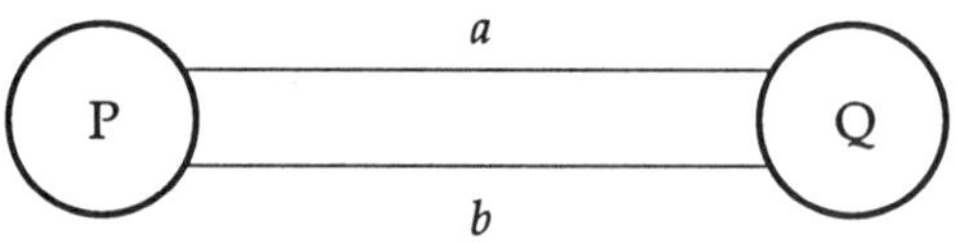

Figure 6.6 Interacting processes potentially in conflict.

Figure 6.6 depicts an interaction graph for a system composed of two processes, *P* and *Q*, which share both events *a* and *b*. Suppose *P* offers its partner *Q* only event *a* upon some state. If *Q* behaves deterministically then it will grant that request and behave accordingly. On the other hand, if *Q* behaves non-deterministically then it may refuse the request and the system deadlocks. (Remember, *Q* is not divergent. Hence, it must offer *b*, which is refused by *P*.) *P* and *Q* are then in conflict. They cannot agree on the order in which shared events occur. Clearly, local protocol has broken down.

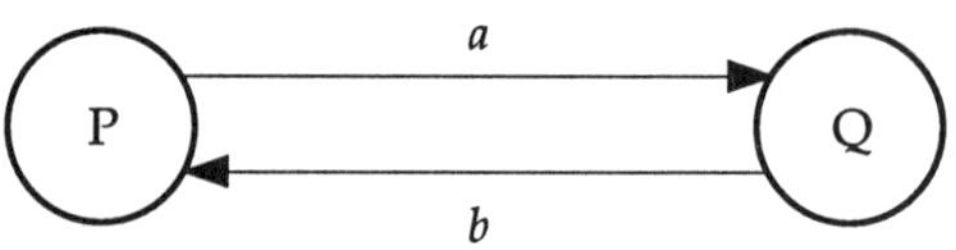

Figure 6.7 Invalid, cyclically dependent, client/server protocol.

Figure 6.7 represents a healthier state of affairs, or so we might think. Local protocol has been "improved", or at any rate rendered more complicated. *Q* has made a prior commitment always to grant a request to engage in *a*, and *P* has made a similar agreement regarding *b*. Each attempts to act as client (or server) to the other. Unfortunately, there are many possible system states and a large proportion of them will be deadlock states. For example, *P* may be ready to engage in just *a*, and *Q* ready to engage in just *b*. This is allowed under condition CS1. However, such a system breaks condition CS2, so we should not be surprised at the possibility of deadlock.

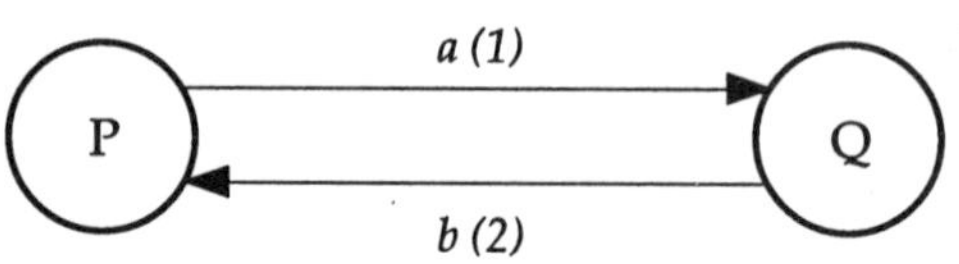

Figure 6.8 Client/server protocol with reflexive service.

Figure 6.8 shows what is needed. An agreement on the explicit ordering must be added to complete the client/server protocol.

CS3 Where multiple events are shared between client and server, the client initiates a finite sequence whose subsequent order must be agreed.

Note that the distinction between client and server has changed. It has become no longer correct to regard *Q* as a client at all. *P* is the *master* of the interaction since it alone may initiate a sequence of events.

We must be careful about precisely what condition CS3 means. In its broadest interpretation it means that at any time the client may request any event which the server undertakes to grant. So begins another sequence, which may *interleave* with others. Notice, though, that a client appears non-deterministic to a server, who cannot control the choice of event which begins a new sequence.

Figure 6.8 may depict the very simplest case, which is in fact equivalent to handshake synchronization if the events concerned are simply signals. In such a system events proceed in lockstep, i.e. they simply alternate (assuming both processes are cyclic).

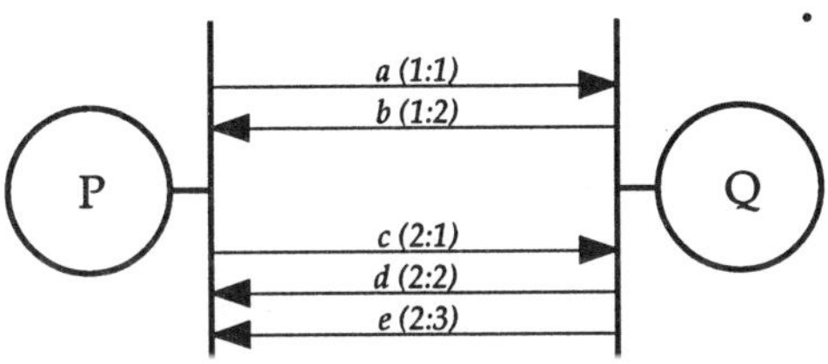

Figure 6.9 Client/server protocol with compound, reflexive service.

Figure 6.9 depicts a more complicated example. Here, there are two possible events which *P* might offer *Q* to initiate a sequence. Once again, this directed interaction graph is an abstraction which does not bind the actual ordering of events very tightly. It represents systems which interleave sequences *and* those which do not. It also leaves *P* free to be decomposed into subordinate processes which may interact in any way keeping with the provisions of the client/server protocol.

Any client/server event sequence may be referred to as a *service*. (An occurrence of such a sequence is regarded as an instance of that service.) To reduce the complexity of representation of this form of abstraction, yet another graph is introduced. A *client/server graph* is identical to the directed interaction graph except that each arc represents the presence and orientation of a *service*. Condition CS2 may be extended to apply to such graphs without amendment. Any system which may be represented by a client/server graph, where each service obeys conditions CS1 and CS3, is guaranteed to be free of deadlock.

A typical application of client/server protocols is to systems which require the layered provision of access to shared resources. An example might be an operating system providing file abstraction to protect persistent memory.

Server implementation: alternation and prioritized alternation

The structure of the procedural implementation of a client need obey no normal form. The form will be dependent upon the application concerned. However, there are normal forms which apply to server implementation regardless of application. Indeed, they prove ubiquitous.

For the sake of brevity, we shall only consider implementations where shared events are distinguished by the synchronous communication channel employed. These will serve to make some important points and raise the relevant issues.

```
WHILE running
  ALT i=0 FOR number.of.inputs
    input[i] ? request
      SEQ
        ... respond to request
```

Listing 6.4 Server implementation using alternative (selection by ready event) construct.

There are two problems with the implementation given in Listing 6.4. First, there is no guarantee of *fairness* in the service provided. A greedy client may cause others to receive no service at all since it may always be ready and waiting when the server becomes ready to serve. We might hope that the semantics of the alternative (ALT) construct would imply an *arbitrary* selection when more than one client is ready. Unfortunately, the realization of such semantics is hard and expensive to achieve in practice, so such hope might well be in vain. We shall consider this problem no further here since it remains one of programming language semantics.

The second problem *is* our concern here. The response to any service-initiating event will occur without interruption until it terminates. In other words request and response will cycle in lockstep fashion. This is rarely what is required in the real world.

Applications which have to interact with the real world face a stark fact of life, *priority*. While it may be possible to realize desktop business applications without dealing with priority, there are very few embedded, real-time, or control applications of software where that remains true. In addition, priority can be exploited to make behaviour deterministic where it would otherwise not be so. Hence, it is often valuable to introduce priority into a design, even where it is not inherent in the application.

```
WHILE running
  PRI ALT i=0 FOR number.of.inputs
    input[i] ? request
      SEQ
        ... respond to request
```

Listing 6.5 Server implementation using prioritized alternative construct.

Listing 6.5 shows a modification of the previous implementation to use a prioritized alternative construct. The semantics of occam's PRI ALT differ only in that events which are listed higher up (of lower index value) are favoured. There is no *pre-emption*. If a higher-priority request arrives before the completion of a response it will simply have to wait. For many applications of client/server protocol this is simply not acceptable.

The subject of pre-emptive scheduling algorithms has traditionally been addressed under the heading of operating systems. Now, in the days of concurrent programming, it is desirable that the implementor of an application should be able to take direct control within a program, in order to meet the requirements of a design. Indeed, the semantics of the PAR construct of the programming language employed should dictate operating system services rather than the other way around.

```
PRI PAR i=0 FOR number.of.inputs
  WHILE running
    SEQ
      input ? request
      ... respond to request
```

Listing 6.6 Server implementation using prioritized parallel construct.

A better normal form for server implementation can be achieved by decomposition. One subordinate process is spawned to respond to each service-initiating event, as shown in Listing 6.6. This time the semantics of the code depend upon those of the prioritized parallel construct of the programming language. If occam's PRI PAR does not offer what we require then we choose, demand, or (heaven forbid) create a programming language which does. In fact, occam should satisfy most such requirements. The semantics of PRI PAR call for the pre-emption of a process by any of higher priority which become ready[8]. Note that this implies the interleaving of services.

The normal form shown in Listing 6.6 might be termed *priority alternation*. A process which directly interacts alternately with a number of partners is said to be *alternating*. Such a process has to resolve the problem of who to respond to first, given a number of partners each demanding attention. Otherwise it may become like the donkey which starves because it is unable to choose between two equally inviting bales of hay. Priority offers the best strategy simply because it will usually be found anyway if sought out in the application domain.

Any programming language worthy of use in programming concurrency should allow the expression of behaviour dictated by priority. Concurrent (or parallel) programming demands a concurrent programming language.

Client/server protocol and Object-Oriented Programming

The fundamental ideas of OOP have been discussed earlier in this text. It has also already been pointed out that communication between concurrent running objects (processes) is understood to be synchronous. In most OOP implementations it is achieved by employing procedure invocation. This has two main advantages. First, OOP may be introduced as an extension of existing popular procedural programming languages. Secondly, hardware support for procedure invocation is provided by all popular processor architectures, usually in the form of a stack.

There is one other advantage to using procedure invocation for interprocess synchronous communication that appears not to be widely appreciated. Every OOP program is thus guaranteed deadlock free. The reason for this is that procedure (or function) invocation obeys a rather strict form of client/server protocol. The procedure is always ready to be called and guarantees termination (and return of result, in the case of a function) within a finite time. OOP is therefore a healthy paradigm for concurrent programming.

There is one disadvantage, however. Procedure invocation limits concurrent programs to a rather confined domain. The particular client/server protocol implied by procedure invocation requires transactions to proceed in strict lockstep. Each client request must be followed by a response before another request may be made. This may be inefficient in some applications.

Failure to recognize the fundamental nature of synchronous communication means that object-oriented design is unnecessarily restrictive. If it is available as a primitive of the programming language then it may be implemented *efficiently* by the compiler. If, in turn, it is available as a primitive of the machine language then *optimum* efficiency may be achieved.

6.3.4 Combining local protocols

Unfortunately, the design rules governing the combination of cyclic ordered processes and client/server protocol within a single system remain a matter for research. It is not as easy as it might at first seem, except for certain very simple cases. For example, a system employing cyclic order protocol and another employing client/server protocol may join via a single channel without much problem. Both design rules may remain valid. However, beyond such a simple case lies danger.

The important point is that there must exist a guarantee of consistent global event ordering. Unless a proof exists that a certain combination of local protocols between neighbours is able to afford such a guarantee then the design cannot be considered valid. Such proofs have been published for both the design rules discussed above.

Let us all hope that we may look forward to the day when software is engineered with the same confidence as are bridges and aircraft. That confidence cannot exist without appropriate design rules which are easily applied by a properly trained engineer, and which possess a solid formal foundation of theory.

Bibliography

There follows a brief sample of the literature on the topic discussed in this chapter. There is a great deal of literature on the subject, and this is not the place for a comprehensive survey. The purpose of this chapter is to provide a tutorial introduction to the subject, and that of this bibliography to guide the interested reader to the next step. The order is purely alphabetical. The order in which the material might be read is a decision which the comments provided should help the reader to make.

Brinch-Hanson, P. 1973. *Operating system principles.* Englewood Cliffs, New Jersey: Prentice Hall.

Origin of client/server protocol. (The author prefers to refer to it as *master/servant* protocol.) The synchronous communication channels used to discuss deadlock consist of *queue* data structures. This makes very little difference to the possibility of deadlock (none if the queue size is unity). After a discussion of the nature of deadlock, the author first presents the protocol in the context of preventing deadlock caused by competition for resource allocation. He then goes on to show how the same method works to prevent communication deadlock.

Dijkstra, E. W. 1965. Co-operating sequential processes. In *Programming languages*, F. Genuys (ed.), 43-112. NewYork: Academic Press.

Where the study of deadlock began. Long before it became a programming issue, it was one of operating system design. Many operating systems relied on human operators to intervene to remove deadlock. Dijkstra was the first to recognize the problem, analyze it effectively, and report his findings.

Dijkstra, E. W. & C. S. Scholten 1982. A class of simple communication patterns. In *Selected writings in computing*, E. W. Dijkstra (ed.), 334-337. Berlin: Springer-Verlag.

Origin of the notion of cyclic ordered processes. Includes a precise, though non-mathematical, account of how they may be combined to guarantee deadlock-freedom.

Hoare, C. A. R. 1985. *Communicating sequential processes*. Englewood Cliffs, New Jersey: Prentice Hall.

This is a book which can turn your perception of computation upside down. Beware, it can also radically change your perception of the world, especially vending machines. The very first sentence of the first chapter invites the reader to forget about computers and programming and think instead about the world. If there really is such a thing as computer science then this seems like the best way to start into it.

The theory of Communicating Sequential Processes (CSP) underlies the view of both parallel systems and of their programming which underlies the entire approach made in this text. The vocabulary of the book is highly mathematical, for the sake of precision, although there is not too much manipulation, and the style of explanation is very readable.

Martin, J., I. East, S. Jassim 1994. Design rules for deadlock freedom. *Transputer Communications* **2**(3), 1–12.

Attempts to build a bridge between the engineering and theoretical approaches to deadlock avoidance, and to provide a hierarchy of design rules which are broadly applicable. It unifies some design rules already known and adds one or two new ones.

Roscoe, A. W. & N. Dathi 1986. *The pursuit of deadlock freedom*. PRG-57, November 1986. Available from Oxford University Computing Laboratory, Oxford University, 8–11 Keble Road, Oxford OX1 3QD, England.

A classic paper on deadlock avoidance whose approach underlies this chapter. It is based on a refinement of what is known as the *failures model* of CSP. It provides a comprehensive theory which provides a very sound basis for the elucidation of design rules, and for reasoning about deadlock with precision.

Welch, P. H., G. Justo & C. Willcock 1993. High-level paradigms for deadlock-free high performance systems. In *Proceedings of Transputer Applications and Systems '93*, R. Grebe et al. (eds), 981-1004. Amsterdam: IOS Press.

Takes an engineering, rather than theoretical, approach. It provides extremely useful design rules for deadlock avoidance in the engineering of systems with Communicating Process Architecture (CPA). It summarizes an earlier paper by one of the authors (Welch) which identified I/O PAR and I/O SEQ processes and showed how they may be used to afford a guarantee of deadlock freedom. It also brings the client/server protocol into the context of modern concurrent programming. The discussion is well illustrated by example. A most valuable contribution is a very lucid account of just how insidious the threat of deadlock can be. It describes a frightening example of a badly designed safety-critical system where failure is rare enough not to be spotted by testing but sufficiently frequent to kill people.

---

1 To "abstract" means to reduce something until it possesses only those features which are *salient* to a certain context or purpose. Ability to abstract varies, but is a key factor of intelligence.

2 "Edge" refers to the association of two nodes where their order has no meaning, and is drawn as a straight line. If their order does possess meaning, and it is to be represented, then the association is referred to as an "arc", which is drawn as an arrow.

3 Long ago, before computers became cheap and ubiquitous, the term "trace" was commonly encountered by programmers. One had to submit a program to acolytes who would run it as soon as the machine they protected became available. The remoteness of the machine made programs unreliable. In order to help diagnose faults, the acolytes would return a trace of the program execution. Nowadays, the term has dropped out of use, which is a shame because it remains useful, particularly in diagnosing program faults.

4 A *rotation* is said to exist wherever an arc exists in both directions between a pair of nodes.

5 A charming story of religious origin seems relevant. A student of ethics asks his teacher, "Master, what are heaven and hell?", to which the teacher gives the following reply. "Hell is a table loaded down with sumptuous food but surrounded by starving people. They can reach the food only by using the forks provided. They cannot feed themselves because the forks are longer than their arms." The student then asks, "Master, what then is heaven?" "Heaven is the very same place, the same table, the same food, and the same people." "How can that be?" asks the worried student. After a little delay, the teacher locks eyes with the student and says, *"In heaven they feed each other!"*

6 A "circuit" in a graph consists of a sequence of distinct nodes which form a *closed path* such that each is visited exactly once without crossing any edge (or arc) more than once.

7 A "trail" in a graph is a connected sequence of edges (or arcs). It is said to be "closed" when the final edge (arc) ends at the same node from which the first begins.

8 Unfortunately, implementations of occam are often limited. That for the Inmos Transputer is limited to just the two levels of priority that its hardware scheduler provide. A compromise made is to "round-robin" time-slice low-priority processes. High-priority processes run until they terminate as, of course, they should.

Index